Anthropology and Disaster in Japan

This book focuses on the 3.11 disaster in Japan, involving a powerful earthquake and tsunami, from an anthropological perspective. It critically reflects on the challenges of conducting anthropological research when encountering disaster at home and the position of social scientist as sufferer. Emphasizing the role of culture in disaster mitigation, the book offers theoretical consideration of the role of cultural heritage in risk management, in line with recent trends in international policy on disaster risk reduction. Taking an approach "with the people in," the author explores how culture features in disaster recovery at community level and considers implications for policy. The chapters explore the response and adaptation by local cultural practitioners and performing arts groups as well as farmers and fishers. Japanese farming and fishing are presented as an innovative and dynamic part of the recovery process. The book will be of interest to scholars and policymakers working in disaster studies, Japan studies, and fields including anthropology, geography, sociology, and heritage management.

Hiroki Takakura is Professor of Social Anthropology at Tohoku University, Japan. He is affiliated with the Center for Northeast Asian Studies and the Graduate School of Environmental Studies.

Routledge Focus on Anthropology

For more information about this series, please visit: www.routledge.com/
anthropology/series/RFA

Anthropology and Disaster in Japan

Cultural Contributions to Recovery after the 2011 Earthquake and Tsunami

Hiroki Takakura

Routledge
Taylor & Francis Group

LONDON AND NEW YORK

First published 2023
by Routledge
4 Park Square, Milton Park, Abingdon, Oxon OX14 4RN

and by Routledge
605 Third Avenue, New York, NY 10158

Routledge is an imprint of the Taylor & Francis Group, an informa business

British Library Cataloguing-in-Publication Data
A catalogue record for this book is available from the British Library

ISBN: 978-1-032-37239-6 (hbk)
ISBN: 978-1-032-39180-9 (pbk)
ISBN: 978-1-003-34875-7 (ebk)

DOI: 10.4324/9781003348757

Typeset in Times New Roman
by Apex CoVantage, LLC

Contents

Figures

Tables

Acknowledgements

Disaster changed my academic life. I never would have thought to write a book on disaster in Japan ten years ago, since my expertise is in Siberian anthropology. As an expert on culture, I intended to support some means of disaster recovery at home for a limited period. Communications with the local people and some accidental sequences of encounter in the scene guided me on the path of disaster anthropology at home, which allowed me to notice how stimulating my vicinity is from ethnographical viewpoint. I could not have completed this book without those fortunate meetings. I first appreciate the people in the field. I would especially like to mention Mr. Takayama Ichio, a farmer and practitioner of the local performing arts.

Institutional supports were indispensable in the completion of this book. My affiliation, Tohoku University, as the closest university from the epicenter, has boosted various academic and practical programs related to the disaster since March 2011, which positively affected the development of my research. One example is the foundation of the International Research Institute of Disaster Science (IRIDeS) as a new department (since 2012); another is the interdepartmental program "Designated National University, Core Research Cluster of Disaster Science" (2016–2021). These two developments gave me chances to exchange not only with disaster social scientists but also with engineers and medical scientists. They changed my views on the application of a more flexible anthropological way on practical matters. Most of the field research in this book was financially backed by this interdepartmental program and the JSPS KAKENHI Grant number 25580179 (2013–2016) and 17K03270 (2017–2020). I also appreciate the financial support for my studies from my department, Center for Northeast Asian Studies, Tohoku University.

Many colleagues and friends have participated in the completion of this book. First, I sincerely appreciate Dr. Sebastien P. Boret for his critical comments on my manuscript. Some of the chapters were presented in seminars or meetings in various places and I would like to thank my colleagues for their critical comments: Kimura Toshiaki, Alyne E. Delaney, Fukuda Yu, Lee Sunhee, Julia Gerster, Kodani Ryusuke, Takizawa Katsuhiko, Tom Gill, Susan Bouterey, Sekiya Yuji, and Yamashita Shinji. Professor Imamura Fumihiko invited me to become involved with the aforementioned interdepartmental program of the university.

Finally, I thank the following publishers and the organization for permission to use portions of my articles and chapters. All of them have been revised, including the titles. I have occasionally added or deleted sections of text and at times changed the framework of discussion to enhance the integrity of the book.

Chapter 2 is based on "The Anthropologist as Both Disaster Victim and Disaster Researcher: Reflections and Advocacy," published in *Crisis and Disaster in Japan and New Zealand: Actors, Victims and Ramifications*, edited by S. Bouterey and L. Marceau, Palgrave-Macmillan, pp. 79–103, 2018.

Chapter 3 is based on "Lessons from Anthropological Projects Related to the Great East Japan Earthquake and Tsunami: Intangible Cultural Heritage Survey and Disaster Salvage Anthropology," published in *World Anthropologies in Practice: Situated Perspectives, Global Knowledge*, edited by J. Gledhill, ASA monograph 52. London: Bloomsbury, pp. 211–224, 2016.

Chapter 4 is based on "The role of intangible cultural heritage in the disaster recovery in Fukushima," published in *Proceedings of the Asia-Pacific Regional Workshop on Intangible Cultural Heritage and Natural Disasters*, edited by W. Iwamoto and Y. Nojima, Osaka: International Research Center for Intangible Cultural Heritage in the Asia-Pacific Region, pp. 81–89, 2019.

Chapter 5 is based on "Local Agricultural Knowledge as Time Manipulation: Paddy Field Farmers after the Great East Japan Earthquake of 2011," published in *Asian Ethnology* 77 (1–2) pp. 257–284, 2018.

Chapter 6 is based on "Individualism and collectivism in small-scale fisheries post-3.11 Japan," published in *Disaster Prevention and Management: An International Journal* 30 (6) pp. 26–38, 2021.

1 Introduction

How can social scientists enter disaster research as affected parties? The purpose of this book is to discuss the challenges and prospects of anthropological studies on disasters as a scientist who has experienced them in his homeland. Scientists must provide unique expertise and transdisciplinary collaboration in a post-disaster setting (Alexander 2012). One of their aims is to explore the role of culture in disaster risk reduction and the way anthropologists engage with it. More recently, the United Nations Office for Disaster Risk Reduction and UNESCO have focused on the relationship between culture and disasters. This manuscript contributes to this line of research by drawing lessons from the Great East Japan Earthquake, the subsequent tsunami, and the explosions at the Fukushima Daiichi Nuclear Power Plant, which occurred on 11 March 2011 and are commonly referred to as the 3.11 disaster.

Disaster anthropology examines the sociocultural process of suffering and reconstruction and makes practical recommendations using the applied approach based on the researcher's fieldwork in the disaster-affected area. It is assumed that anthropologists should have had a long commitment to the people and place before the disaster (Hoffman and Oliver-Smith 2002; Shimizu 2017). However, when an anthropologist faces a disaster at home without regional expertise, what type of research can this scholar do? This question is based on my personal experience, but it can be applied to any anthropologist or social scientist.

The book elaborates on my initial dilemma and subsequent connections with some theoretical questions. In the complex context of criticism and expectations toward science after the 3.11 disaster, I started my university's documentation project, followed by the intangible cultural heritage project commissioned by the government in the neighboring but unknown local communities through various encounters and coincidences. This starting process reflects the specificity of anthropological knowledge and some

DOI: 10.4324/9781003348757-1

aspects of the perception of anthropology as a scientific discipline by people and public institutions. I adopt an ethnographic approach to explain the destruction and restoration of livelihoods, focusing on local cultural practitioners, farmers, and fishers.

1.1 Culture as a barrier or a facilitator

Why is culture important for disaster risk reduction? Some may think that physical measures, such as tsunami walls, infrastructure, and medical facilities are more effective in reducing disaster risk. These are the so-called "universal models" of disaster risk reduction that focus on the safety of life and the economy. A Japanese civil disaster engineer, Norio Maki, doubts this applicability. The universal model is intended only for the middle class in developed countries and not for the rest of the world (Maki 2015).

I call the different positions provided by cultural models "alternative visions." A relativist approach stresses the importance of local ways of reducing risk. This approach is based on a specific way of thinking about disasters and risks, wherein scientists deny the concept of "natural disaster." If a tsunami appeared in some location without humans, it would not produce damage or loss. Humanity creates disasters. While the relativist scientists choose the term "natural hazard" to indicate the immense magnitude of natural phenomena such as tsunami, earthquake, and eruption, disaster means anthropogenic catastrophe, damage, or loss as a result of human choices (Kelman 2020). The choice is embedded in society and culture. Another scholar explains that "people are not just vulnerable to hazards, but hazards are increasingly the result of human activity" (Oliver-Smith 2015, 548).

The concept of risk involves a sociocultural process, the origin of which goes back to the 1980s. The influential British symbolic anthropologist Mary Douglas emphasized that risk is a social process and/or a cultural construction. She insisted that cultures select different human behaviors that correspond to a similar range of hazards and the predicament can be experienced through a "culturally fabricated lens" (Douglas and Wildavsky 1983). Some social scientists follow this idea, with the critique that culture does not always prescribe risk cognition and behavior but generates new alternatives. The social scientists who followed them also emphasized the perspectives of gender and social inequality. In addition, their arguments are more contentious because they go beyond the social sciences to practical disaster policy or interdisciplinary fields, including physical and medical sciences or transdisciplinary attitudes (Alexander 2012; Gaillard et al. 2015; Ichinosawa 2010; Oliver-Smith 2013a).

Here is a critical argument: culture is either a barrier or a facilitator to disaster risk reduction (Kulatunga 2010; Kruger et al. 2015). The catalyst for focusing on the role of culture in disaster risk reduction was the 2004 India-Sumatra earthquake and tsunami. Villagers who had local knowledge about tsunamis survived, while immigrants and tourists who did not perished, underscoring the value of culture in disaster survival (Shaw et al. 2008). On the other hand, different religions or beliefs, which are inseparable parts of culture, produce different interpretations of loss and damage from disasters (Falk 2010; Merli 2010). For example, such beliefs may lead to a strong attachment to a particular place related to the ancestors, which becomes a barrier to evacuation. Udayangani Kulatunga, a social scientist who studies disasters in Sri Lanka, emphasized that culture has the power to either increase or decrease the vulnerability of communities to disasters (Kulatunga 2010). Other scholars have also argued for the cultural embeddedness of disaster risk. The focus on the sociocultural process of disaster risk reduction (how people perceive, experience, and respond to it) can help us understand why people are affected by hazards, which allows us to consider how they minimize the impact of hazards (Bankoff et al. 2015).

After the end of the Cold War, a similar tone accompanied the discussion in the field of economic development. Samuel Huntington posed the thought-provoking question of whether culture matters for social development rather than political ideology. He asked, "If they do, how can cultural obstacles to economic and political development be removed or changed to facilitate progress?" (Huntington 2000, xiv). Policy science scholars indicate that the argument for the universality of policy and the role of culture is repeatedly disputed in resource distribution issues in the contemporary world (Hodgson and Irving 2007). The issue in disaster risk reduction might be a different version of the same issue. In addition, I assert that culture is regarded as an object for the manipulation of these implementations.

1.2 Study "with the people in"

Culture is important for disaster preparedness. Understanding disaster and viewing risk through a cultural lens leads to local perceptions and experiences to find local needs and appropriate actions. It also helps to build trust between those affected and policymakers or scientists. These are the main reasons for focusing on culture in disaster risk reduction.

However, I wonder whether scientists or policymakers should remove or change the culture for the sake of disaster risk reduction. If one takes the universal approach, they do not hesitate to modify some cultural behavior or think of it as an obstacle to risk reduction. However, how does the scholar of a cultural (revisionist) approach decide? As far as they explore the social vulnerabilities against disaster, they might recommend modifications to the community or society concerned in a cultural manner. The contemporary influential British anthropologist Tim Ingold insists on anthropology as a "philosophy with the people in" by "taking others seriously" (Ingold 2018, 4). These anthropologists must refrain from evaluating different cultures from their own points of view. They understand "the depth of difference that may exist in the views of their neighbors" (Hendry 2016, 29). It may be understandable that a certain behavior, based on local culture, increases vulnerability to hazards and, therefore, should be changed. However, who deserves an assessment of vulnerability? What contexts should one identify as vulnerability (or resilience)? Vulnerability assessment changes depending on the periodic condition (short or long term), population size (small community or larger city), and positioning (including political ideology and economic thinking) of the assessor.

As an anthropologist who faced a disaster at home, honestly, I could take neither the universal model nor the cultural approach that uncover the barriers of culture for disaster risk reduction. I do not deny the social significance of this cultural approach. However, I want to find out how culture has enabled people to rebuild communities at the site of the disaster. Rather than scientifically analyzing the vulnerability of society to determine preparedness, I focus on the recovery process based on people. I try to study the capacities of the affected people and their environment. The study "with the people in" is the basis of my approach for this book.

1.3 Japanese viewpoints

Many anthropologists in Japan somehow shared this approach when confronted with the site of the 3.11 disaster. By "Japanese" here I do not mean ethnicity, but rather the people who work mainly in Japanese science. One Japanese anthropologist, who recognized the intellectual colonialism created by the foreign mass media networks after the disaster, tried to construct the dialogic space between the two "homes" of Japan and the United States (Wood 2012). In this context, a giant disaster leads scholars to tempt the gold rush of post-disaster research, which might produce intellectual hegemony (Gaillard and Gomez 2015; Numazaki 2012). However, many anthropologists in Japan have begun to recognize the power of anthropology as a slow science that avoids "grandstand games" and focuses slowly and carefully on the human aspects of a disaster (Yamashita 2012). Tom Gill and his group first published a collective monograph of survivor ethnography in Japanese (Gill et al. 2013a) and later in English (Gill et al. 2013b). They demonstrated the importance of ethnography with anthropological thoughts immediately after a disaster or another unknown social process. They explained that these seemingly extraordinary and temporary behaviors could be understood from a cultural perspective, or they interpreted that others needed to open new pathways "against culture" (Abu-lughod 1996). Several anthropologists reported that community development worked with local people, administration, and non-governmental organizations (Takezawa 2013, 2016) to secure the local kind of dignity as an important element of post-disaster human security (Uchio 2016, 2018).

Accordingly, scholars have examined the role of intangible cultural heritage in post-disaster recovery (Hashimoto and Hayashi 2016; Takakura and Takizawa 2013; Takakura and Yamaguchi 2018; Takakura et al. 2012). Some have also argued that local performing arts contributed to local recovery, explaining their role in shaping social cohesion and a sense of local belonging in relieving as well as alleviating grief (Hayashi 2012; Lahournat 2016).

Another colleague focused on disaster memories, which formed "hierarchies of affectedness" to disrupt social cohesion (Gerster 2019). Therefore, the government and people require public disaster memorials. Some examined the function that contributes to the alleviation of sorrow and the collective identity required for survivors. In particular, these scholars have dared to make policy recommendations based on their recognition of the importance of memorial diversity, whether through traditional religious memorials or new inventions that meet the many needs of mourners and the bereaved, in both old and new generations (Boret and Shibayama 2016; Boret and Shibayama 2018).

1.4 Methodology

The approach of studying a phenomenon "with the people in" examines how local culture and people's skills contribute to disaster recovery. In my opinion, anthropologists should first determine the functions of local tradition, knowledge, wisdom, and innovation in a post-disaster setting. Second, they should promote these values not only to local people but also to policymakers. The results of studies with local people are needed to inform national and international policymakers in developing better ways to reduce post-disaster risk.

The policies are not simple governmental tools but agencies creating social relations and new domains of people, objects, and institutions (Shore 2012; Shore and Wright 2011). They are the most effective tools for shaping contemporary routines (Jenkins 2007). In this sense, anthropological findings in the post-disaster setting should be translated/edited to policy recommendations. I believe that the combination of insightful ethnography focused on local ways of coping with disasters and the corresponding policy recommendations make an irreplaceable anthropological contribution to post-disaster risk reduction, which is the methodology of this book.

The unique feature of this study is the sufferer's perspective, the author's participant observation, and the use of unstructured interviews with local communities over a relatively long period. The study began in May 2011 and ended in March 2020, and the geographical area of the field research was mainly in Miyagi and Fukushima, Japan. This book highlights the cultural resilience of local cultural practitioners, farmers, and fishers in Japan. It challenges the conventional view of these people, showing them to be more innovative and dynamic in the adaptation process of recovery. Also, it provides theoretical implications on the role of culture in disaster risk management.

1.5 The composition of this book

Chapter 2 is titled "The anthropologist as both victim and disaster researcher." It asks how anthropologists should respond to disasters in their hometowns. When one is both a disaster researcher and a victim of the same disaster, the scope of response can be limited in the immediate aftermath; however, this dual role can ensure a deep insider's perspective.[1] I describe some practical difficulties faced by such researchers and their advantages, based on my experiences of the 3.11 disaster and my role as leader of the Tohoku University project aimed at recording and archiving the narratives of the university-related people who experienced the earthquake. This study explored the academic and social significance of the project and considered the role of anthropologists as citizens in their native countries.

Chapter 3, "Reflections from a survey of post-disaster intangible cultural heritage," examines the contribution of anthropologists' activism to the affected region and its communities. It explores the question of what kind of social engagement anthropologists' responses represent and examines the related impact that anthropologists' activities have on the public. This chapter addresses the question of how to conduct an intangible cultural heritage survey project in an anthropological context. It argues that the heritage survey in disaster-stricken areas can be part of the inventory of research methods in the field of anthropology.

Chapter 4, titled "The structural time in the folk performing arts," addresses the specific local cultural heritage in Fukushima to explore the reasons for its contribution to disaster recovery. Group activities such as the *Soma-Nagareyama* dance in Futaba Township and traditional performing arts in Iwaki City were used to examine the ways in which affected communities reflected on the past and on their social impacts. Why does cultural tradition provide people with a sense of recovery? The key seems to be the structural time embedded in intangible cultural heritage. I identify the concept, borrowed from Evans-Pritchard (1969) canonical work, *The Nuer*, and argue for the possibility of a disaster risk reduction policy.

Two chapters deal with local knowledge of agriculture and fishing. Chapter 5, titled "The strategies of the paddy farmers with indigenous knowledge," examines the role of farmers' local knowledge in the context of adapting to a post-disaster situation. The 3.11 disaster damaged Japan's northeastern coastal region and devastated all human spaces, including agricultural fields. Many small-scale farmers gave up cultivation, and the government supported large-scale farmers. Those who resumed rice cultivation expanded their land acreage. I examine this sociocultural context, focusing on the dynamics and complexity of farmers' local knowledge. The most important aspect of this knowledge is time manipulation, which contributes to labor efficiency. Local knowledge has three dimensions: the maturation process, the environment, and the biological response. While the first two are oriented toward tradition and collectivity, the latter is rather individualistic and innovative. Embracing these three types of knowledge in communities supports agricultural adaptation in the post-disaster context.

Chapter 6, titled "The norms of recovery among small-scale fisheries," investigates the context of post-disaster cooperation among independent small-scale fishers in Miyagi. The corresponding post-disaster cooperation among fishers is not a mere "disaster utopia" but is embedded in the socio-ecological context of fisheries. Both individual and group fisheries have devolved. They have institutionalized a competitive allocation for sedentary fish with low resource fluctuation, whereas an equal-outcome allocation is assumed for migratory fish with high resource fluctuation. These strategies form a fishing continuum that connects competitive individualism with collectivism in the community, contributing to resilience in disaster recovery. The multifaceted resource strategy that features family-based occupational differentiation in a community is crucial for small-scale fishers.

In the final chapter, concluding thoughts on the role of culture in disaster risk reduction are presented.

Note

1 One might be reminded of the native anthropological debate (Kuwayama 2004); however, I do not take up the issue in this book. Certainly, I was born and grew up in Japan, but I had never studied Japanese culture professionally until the 3.11 disaster. In addition, it seems unwise to think that one should be a native anthropologist because the one grows up in that land, particularly in the globalized contemporary world.

2 The anthropologist as both victim and disaster researcher

2.1 Anthropologists and disasters

Anthropologists often begin disaster research by chance, as disasters are unexpected events. When anthropologists are confronted with a disaster that has occurred in a place with which they are familiar or in a place that is connected to their fieldwork, they inevitably begin research, both practically and scientifically (Gill et al. 2013b; Hayashi 2010; Itani 1982; Shimizu 2001). First, they would view the events as "natural occurrences, accidents, bad luck" (Oliver-Smith 2013b, 276). However, soon they recognize that the disaster presents a rare opportunity for researchers to understand the sociocultural response of a particular society in an extreme situation (Hoffman and Oliver-Smith 2002, 14). This can lead to uncovering aspects of the sociocultural processes of a particular society and the ability to gain a deeper and more comprehensive understanding of the interaction between humans and their environment. Furthermore, anthropological approaches to disasters provide many practical measures to aid the recovery of affected communities (Maki and Hayashi 1999; Maki and Yamamoto 2015).

A disaster can strike any place where an anthropologist lives and works. If a person experiences a disaster at home, the researcher may also be a victim. How should one respond to disasters that have occurred at home?

In this chapter, I report my own experiences as an anthropologist and reflect on such questions. I take the approach of "reflective ethnography," a method that emphasizes subjectivity and awareness of one's role as an ethnographer who culturally translates a focused setting (Barnard 2000, 35). First, I describe my own practical situation after the 3.11 disaster and, then, I consider the event as a researcher. I was asked to organize an archiving project for the earthquake. This chapter explores the academic and social significance of that project and considers the role of the anthropologist as a citizen at home.

DOI: 10.4324/9781003348757-2

Immediately after the 3.11 disaster, there was a situation that could be described as a gold mine of scientific knowledge for disaster recovery policies (Ishikawa 2011). Every researcher recognized that somehow their expertise should be able to contribute to assisting the victims and their local communities. During this period, researchers often volunteered or were asked by others to help or contribute to recovery in some way, both as general members of society and as individuals with specialized knowledge. Economists, clinical psychologists, medical doctors, civil engineers, and geologists contributed their expertise to the affected regions. Some anthropologists, in collaboration with historians and folklorists, offered practical help to local communities concerning cultural heritage recovery and conservation policies (Hidaka 2012; Hashimoto 2015).

However, many anthropologists in Japan were reluctant to participate in actions similar to those mentioned previously, even though they wanted to provide their expertise for the benefit of the survivors (Kimura 2013, 14). I think that the main reason for this is that while anthropologists are certainly legitimate cultural specialists, their methodology depends heavily on the precise knowledge of the local culture and language in a given place. A Japanese anthropologist who speaks Japanese may not know the local dialects, and while they may know the basic cultural facts of a certain region, this knowledge might be based only on experience, education, and sources from the media, such as books and television. In other words, the knowledge and language required are strictly geo-culturally defined, especially in the initial stages of responding to a disaster. Mutual trust between researchers and subjects strongly influences the success of participant observation and unstructured interviews. These methods may be inappropriate for anthropological field research following an extreme disaster when the anthropologist is unfamiliar with the site.

Japanese anthropologists conduct field research worldwide, and the number of researchers who specialize in work outside of Japan has far outnumbered anthropologists who study Japanese culture (Kuwayama 2004; Shimizu 2001). Researchers may have a unique systematic method of studying a particular culture from an academic standpoint but lack local knowledge of a region in their own country. This was typical of many Japanese anthropologists after the 3.11 disaster. It is easy to imagine that anthropologists feel the responsibility as academic professionals to respond to a disaster as academic specialists and recognize the ability of their discipline to make an important social contribution (Hayashi et al. 2016). However, their expertise may be insufficient or inadequate at the site of the disaster. One anthropologist warns in his autoethnography (Kawaguchi 2019) that there is a tendency to ignore local cultural differences among "Japanese." This situation could be repeated in the home country of any anthropologist affected by such a disaster. Therefore, this study aims to explore what can be done by such researchers in the face of natural hazards.

2.2 My situation post-quake

Regarding my personal experience as an anthropologist, six months after the quake, I was funded by the local government to lead a project on local intangible cultural heritage and community resilience. Subsequently, I devoted my full energy and expertise to the project (Takakura and Takizawa 2014). However, in the first few months after the earthquake, it was difficult for me to find something to do as a researcher. In addition to the ethical and sociocultural issues discussed later, I felt guilty because both my house and my workplace had been spared from severe damage. My house had virtually no physical damage, except for the interruption of gas and water supply for about a month; electricity was restored after three days. Tohoku University, where I work, is the university closest to the epicenter of the earthquake; however, it is not close to the area affected by the tsunami. Although some campus buildings were severely damaged and some people associated with the university lost their lives, the college semester was only postponed by one month.

My life and work were manageable, though fraught with unfamiliar difficulties. However, I was constantly confronted with the terrible reality that I saw in the newspapers and on the TV about what was happening in the tsunami-affected areas. Some areas severely damaged by the tsunami were familiar to me from my family vacations. Still, I had never done research there, and I was hesitant to visit temporary shelters in these affected regions to do research. I began to exchange ideas with my colleagues and some students, and I thought about the possibility of recording the experiences of these people using anthropological research methods. Embarking on participant observation fieldwork in this context would be disrespectful to the survivors. Some anthropologists went into the disaster-affected area as volunteers (Slator 2015; Takezawa 2013). What could and should I do as an anthropologist was a serious question that troubled me for several months beginning in early May 2011. One answer to this question lead to the Toshinroku Project described in the following section. I believe that this type of project, focused on an organization from an insider's point of view, can provide valuable information for anthropologists who experience disasters and other such catastrophes on the ground.

2.3 The Toshinroku Project in progress

This section describes the Toshinroku Project process and discusses its potential. As will be evident from the discussion, there are several key issues in the project. The first concerns the way an anthropologist interacts with and involves members of their community, in this case, the university community. The second concerns the importance of recording the social reconstruction process in areas that were not affected by the worst destruction.

2.3.1 Outline

When an earthquake with an epicenter off the Pacific coast of the Tohoku region hit at 2:46 p.m. on 11 March 2011, it was immediately followed by a massive tsunami. Where were the people associated with Tohoku University at that time? How did they experience it? Through what sequence of events did they eventually find their way back to normal life at the university? The goal of the Toshinroku Project was to gather the experiences of individuals during and after the disaster and then to share these archives with others. Individuals included students, university faculty members, administrators, employees of the campus store, and other university-related facilities and employees of the companies working with the university in various fields, even people who happened to be visiting the campus at the time of the earthquake.

The reports were collected by a loose group of Tohoku University faculty members and student volunteers at meetings held mainly on campus. At meetings held during the noon recess or in the early evening, participants introduced themselves and talked about their experiences. Other records were obtained through personal interviews. From May to October 2011, the project team heard the stories of nearly 100 people from various perspectives. The transcription of their experiences totaled more than 600 pages in Japanese (equivalent to approximately 108,000 English words).

2.3.2 Commencement

March 11 coincided with the spring break period for students in Japan; therefore, most students, some faculty members, and other staff were not on campus. Immediately after the disaster, both university faculty and administrative staff had to make sure that the students, faculty, and campus were safe. As a result of the strong shaking, books, documents, and scientific equipment fell to the floor and were damaged or destroyed. The damage needed to be cataloged, and, where possible, repairs were made. Some buildings were heavily damaged and no one was allowed to go inside them. The university decided that those who worked in these buildings would work from home until 31 March. The Japanese academic calendar started on 1 April, but Tohoku University deemed that the entire month of April 2011 would be needed to restore the campus and prepare for the new semester. The annual ceremony for new students entering the university was postponed until 6 May, and soon afterward, the semester began.

Since the building that housed my office was one of the most heavily damaged in the university, the administration decided that it could not be used. I had to work from home throughout March, and then in April, I moved to a temporary office on campus with some of my books and a laptop computer. After the first few weeks after the earthquake, life and work on campus were somehow able to continue, in part because electricity, gas, and water were soon restored. Although at this time I was still stuck at home, I began to think about the role of the anthropologist at the site of a disaster. It was psychologically and ethically difficult for me to go to the affected coastal regions. It was also impossible to visit Fukushima because of the explosion at the Fukushima Daiichi Nuclear Power Plant. The regions that were most heavily affected by the tsunami were still far from being stable. TV and newspaper broadcasts were sent from the gymnasiums of local schools, many of which were being used as temporary evacuation sites. Some gymnasiums were also temporary mortuaries, where survivors searched for missing family members (Suzuki, I. 2012; Takezawa 2016).

I was puzzled about whether I could or should find people to interview under the conditions following this disaster. Anthropology is the study of people in terms of their otherness, while ethnography is the art of describing these groups. Should field research be ethically permitted for the sake of science? The reason for my hesitation was the social criticism of academia and journalism toward survivors. I could not find a legitimate reason for field research on shelters. I almost abandoned my attempt at anthropological research in the tsunami-affected region because I had not established relationships with local people before the disaster. On the other hand, I gradually came to recognize the social and academic significance of recording the experiences of survivors. I struggled to find appropriate words to explain the purpose of my field interviews under such extreme conditions to unfamiliar interviewees. I eventually reached two conclusions: one was that applied research with practical purposes might justify going to a particular location hit by a natural hazard, and the second relates to the process of archiving the experiences of members of my own community. Certainly, the university area was subject to less damage than the region hit by the tsunami; however, if population and diversity of people and location[1] were taken into consideration, I believed the experiences of the individuals connected to the university needed to be recorded and archived.

During April 2011, when the university was preparing to reopen, I communicated with many different people, allowing me to speak with others who shared my concerns. Some people were deeply sympathetic to my idea of collecting the narratives of people at the university during and following the earthquake. Several days after the start of the first semester, I called a few people with whom I had spoken to organize a meeting. Associate Professor Kimura Toshiaki and post-doctoral researcher Takizawa Katsuhiko, both from the Department of Religious Studies, and Seki Minako, a student from the Department of Cultural Anthropology, agreed to participate in the first meeting, which was held over lunch at the university. The purpose of this first meeting was to determine the feasibility of a recording project and then, if we decided to proceed, to discuss the purpose and methodology of the project.

We agreed that the project should be undertaken and subsequently decided on a few key themes for the interviews. These included the following questions:

1. Where were people at the time the earthquake struck?
2. What did they first hear and see?
3. How did they react to the disaster?
4. When did they return to the university?

We wanted to approach various individuals connected to the university for these interviews. We settled on six categories of potential interviewees:

1. Domestic students
2. Foreign students
3. Faculty and scholars (including post-doctoral researchers and visiting professors)
4. Administrative staff
5. The staff at the university cafeteria and stores
6. Visitors to the university (for example, vendors who might be meeting researchers, other persons who might be visiting the campus for business, or guest researchers)

It was decided that the interviews would be recorded in group sessions, where participants could tell their stories and listen to others. These sessions could be organized over lunchtime or after class. The most important issue for me at this meeting was deciding on the project's name. Since these were voluntary, interdepartmental activities involving both students and professors, the project name had a performative effect on the embodiment of the activities. We named the project "Tohoku University Disaster Project: Recording Personal Experiences," and gave it the abbreviation "Toshinroku," referring to the original title in Japanese.[2]

The decision to use group sessions for the interviews was partially based on clinical psychology methods, in which participants recount and share their hardships and experiences (Kawai and Washida 2010). This type of interaction promotes a deeper understanding of the contexts in which participants find themselves and has been shown to give speakers a sense of healing. Therefore, we decided that the interviews should be participatory and interactive.

When we began the first trials, which were conducted with individuals from the aforementioned categories and some of their friends and acquaintances, we recognized that the opportunity to share the experience involved not only a sense of healing but also more critical implications for the participants. The atmosphere within the university, particularly for faculty and administrative staff, had been one of chaotic reconstruction. It was difficult for many people to reflect on their own experiences with colleagues and friends on campus because many things needed to be done in preparation for the start of the semester. The group session provided an opportunity for reflection among university scholars and staff as well as an opportunity to understand the different experiences of all involved. We recognized that the group sessions created an alternative time and space for the individual interviewees, away from the pressure to help the university recover from the disaster.

2.3.3 Visiting group sessions as a window of opportunity

The lunch meetings were successful in the first phase. They were organized once or twice a week. The project's initiators invited their friends and colleagues to the sessions, and some of them also introduced their acquaintances. However, we soon encountered various problems. One was the shortage of time: one hour at lunchtime was not enough for all group members to speak and listen. At most, two people were able to tell their stories to a group of typically four to five participants. The second problem was related to the culturally based reluctance of the participants.[3] Some people expressed interest in the project and attended the meetings. They listened to the stories of other members but did not want to talk about their experiences in front of strangers. In addition, administrators' work schedules were not as flexible as those of faculty or students, which affected their ability to attend short lunchtime meetings.

We continued these sessions for several weeks and then had difficulty finding new participants for the reasons stated previously. At this time, Professor Imamura Fumihiko, from the School of Engineering, proposed a visit to his laboratory to hold a group session. Professor Imamura is an internationally recognized scientist who conducts research on tsunami risk reduction engineering. I did not know him at the time, but a colleague approached him about our project. He supported us and volunteered to host these new group meetings.

Three project team members visited the laboratory on 7 June 2011, where almost 20 people (professors, researchers, and students) waited. We divided the participants into three groups and held group sessions, each supervised by a project member. From our previous experience with these sessions, we had learned that it was easier for participants to share their stories with familiar friends and colleagues.

These "visiting sessions" represented a turning point. While we still organized regular lunchtime sessions, we searched for group sessions at laboratories or departments via various friends or colleagues. When these sessions were organized, a benevolent atmosphere developed among the members that encouraged further openness in storytelling.

2.4 Management of the Toshinroku Project

2.4.1 Flexibility

In the first phase of the project, Kimura Toshiaki and I, as project leaders, took turns as chairperson and stenographer. The group meetings began with the chair briefly explaining the purpose of the project, followed by brief self-introductions by each member. Then the chair asked who wanted to speak first. The lunchtime sessions lasted only one hour; therefore, the allocated time for each person was 15–20 minutes.

When one person began to speak, the other participants listened to the story and the stenographer wrote down the narrative on a laptop. Since the project members were not trained stenographers, meeting participants were asked to speak more slowly than usual. The stenographers then simultaneously typed the stories. All participants were given registration cards (Figure 2.1) during the session, which asked for brief personal information. Two or three days after the conclusion of a session, a transcript of the narrative was e-mailed to each person who had spoken during the session. Participants were then asked to confirm the content (Figure 2.2). Speakers were asked to revise the transcripts in case of errors.

As these sessions progressed, some faculty members and students who became actively engaged with this project gradually emerged. Subsequently, some of these individuals were asked to act as chairpersons or stenographers. During this process, various rules for managing sessions were established. First, the chair wrote a report for each meeting (Figure 2.3). In addition, standards for storing and naming electronic files as well as several other minor details that had to be observed were established (Figure 2.4).

Date (YY/MM/DD)	
Name	
Sex	
Age	
Affiliation	
Position	
Hometown	
Whereabouts at time of Quake	
First food eaten after the Quake	
E-mail address	
Telephone	
Publication of your interview text	Yes No All texts will remain anonymous

Figure 2.1 Registration card given to the participants

In addition, all project team members and volunteers were allowed to talk during these group sessions. One student designed a logo for the project and later used her logo for promotional and informational flyers. In July, the respondents were expanded to include merchants who visited the campus regularly, people who visited the campus, and people who happened

Dear Ms. Mr. XXXX,
CC: X (Stenographer), Takakura Hiroki, Kimura Toshiaki (Leaders of the Project)

Thank you for sharing your disaster experiences in a session of our Toshinroku Project. As we advised at the time, we are also collecting records of personal interviews. Please find attached a file providing shorthand notes of your narrative at the session. Please read it carefully and confirm that the content is accurate. If you need to revise the content, please rewrite accordingly.

This manuscript is for archiving. If we plan in future to publish your text, we will consult you on the matter. We would be grateful if you could give your confirmation and return any revisions within two weeks.

The following URL is for the website of our project where you can see what is in progress.
http://toushinroku.blog.fc2.com/

If you are willing to assist us with our project activities, please don't hesitate to contact us.

X (Chairperson)

Figure 2.2 Sample form of the confirmation letter sent to interviewees

Session Report Sheet	
	(For Chairperson Use)
Name of Chairperson	
Date of Session	
Venue of Session	
Number of Participants	
Name of Speaker and Affiliation	(1) (2) (3) (4) (5) (6)
Summary and Comments	

Figure 2.3 Session report sheet

1. Session Report Sheet
<Date Session_report> For example "110623Session_Report" means the session report of 23
June 2011. Saved as "txt."

2. Shorthand Text in Session
<Date_rep_Stenographer's name> For example "110610_rep_Kimura" means the shorthand
texts of multiple interviewees recorded by Kimura on the date of 10 June 2011. Saved as "txt."

3. Shorthand Text for the Interviewee
<Date_interviewee> For example "110714_Hino" means the shorthand text of the narration by
Mr. Hino (pseudonym). This will be sent to Mr. Hino for confirmation of the contents. Saved as
"txt."

4. Shorthand Text for the Interviewee with Confirmation
<Date_interviewee_v2> For example "110714_Hino_v2" means the shorthand text of the
narration by Mr. Hino (pseudonym) with the contents already confirmed. Saved as "txt."

Figure 2.4 Guidelines for saving and naming electronic files

to be on campus on the day of the disaster. As a result, a new system for
in-person interviews by appointment was implemented. From August to
September 2011, when the university was closed for the summer break,
only visiting group sessions and personal interviews were conducted. The
last visiting session was held on 4 October 2011, at the Onagawa Fisheries
Field Station, which is located in a nearby coastal area that was severely
damaged by the tsunami.

The participants' e-mail addresses were registered and added to a mailing
list, which was the main means of communication between the interviewees
in the sessions and project team members. The lunchtime meetings were
usually held in the same room, and most project matters could be discussed
directly after these meetings. In addition, the steering committee met every
two months, and all members were welcome to attend. The more meetings
and interviews that were organized and the more narratives collected, the
less time project team members had to devote to understanding the project
activities. Time was needed to consider moving forward in a different context from group meetings and interviews.

Another tool used to implement the project was the creation of blogs.
Some graduate students had the idea of creating a blog to record the activities of the project, after which the chairperson posted a brief report to the
blog site. This enabled project team members who did not regularly participate in the sessions or who missed a session to follow the project's progress.
The blog was a helpful tool that allowed team members to record the progress of our activities and to share information.

2.4.2 Sharing the narratives

For nearly six months, from May to October 2011, sessions were held to record people's experiences of the disaster, as told by people at the university. A total of 29 sessions were organized at various locations on campus. 92 people signed up to share their experiences. In the project's initial stages, trial sessions were conducted and stories from ten different people were heard. Throughout the project, almost a hundred people had their stories recorded.

As the number of interviews increased and narrative transcripts were collected, the project leaders were confronted with the question of how to share these memories. At the beginning of the project, there was no specific plan for sharing or publishing. As shown previously, the various types of meetings and interviews rapidly increased from mid-June onward, as many volunteers willingly participated in organizing activities. Therefore, a new rule was introduced that required the chair of each meeting to write a report. These reports were published through a closed membership blog website. It was difficult, even for the project leaders, to grasp the process of these sessions in progress and to finalize transcripts of narratives, as they were simultaneously engaged in organizing sessions and recording, transcribing, and archiving the narratives.

In the first few weeks after the beginning of the project, it was thought these narratives could be shared easily; printed versions of checked transcripts could be delivered to departmental offices or they could be brought to lunchtime sessions, which would be sufficient. As mentioned previously, however, the number of transcriptions far exceeded the team's original expectations and totaled approximately 600 pages.

The length of each narrative varied greatly because the time available to the speakers varied in each session. Speakers were asked not only to review the transcripts but also to revise them or add notes. Some participants wrote additional memories after thinking about the text. After the sessions were completed in early October 2011, the core project members began to consider how to share these narratives. In mid-October, Professor Kimura Toshiaki and I read all the transcripts in one day (from lunch to the midnight). We decided that these narratives should be collected into a single manuscript and published as a book (Takakura and Kimura 2012).

2.4.3 Statistics

Because of length limitations, the recorded manuscripts are not cited in this chapter. Instead, this section provides an overview of the narratives and a consideration of the trends expressed by the participants. The statistics in the following section provide general information about the project participants.[4]

Respondents were required to complete a registration card at each session. A total of 92 individuals submitted registration cards; 58 were male and 34 were female. In terms of age, 44% of participants were aged 20–29, 22% were aged 30–39, 20% were aged 40–49, and 14% were aged 50–69. The largest number of participants were Japanese students (30%) and administrators (30%). This was followed by faculty members (21%), international students (11%), and visitors and vendors (8%). The project team tried to avoid biases based on gender, ethnicity, age, and occupation. An effort was made to collect narratives from international students. This provided a very important account of how people coped with disasters. At the time of the disaster, the mass media had critically reported that foreigners were returning to their home countries as a fleeing (escaping) phenomenon (Cadwell 2019). Most students had to return to their home countries. Some international students chose to stay at the university to continue their studies or to participate in volunteer activities in the heavily damaged areas. University personnel were more concerned that international students might not return to the university. These records show the importance of focusing on people as individuals when considering their responses to a disaster.

A quarter of the participants were from the Miyagi prefecture. Tohoku (excluding Miyagi), Kanto (around Tokyo), and Chubu (around Nagoya) regions each accounted for approximately 15% of the participants. Approximately 14% of the respondents were from abroad. The large number of survey participants from Miyagi reflects people's behavior at the university immediately after the disaster; whether foreign or domestic, if one had a "home" apart from Miyagi, people tended to return there. Many narratives described the communication between Miyagi and the participants' hometowns.

Participants asked where they were at the time of the earthquake: 74% were in Miyagi, 21% were in other places in Japan, and 5% had heard about or seen coverage of the disaster while abroad. All university staff and some students outside Miyagi immediately thought of returning to campus. The narratives described the practical difficulties and moral dilemmas they faced, especially after the explosion at the Fukushima Daiichi Nuclear Power Plant.

Based on the information collected in the archives, the book's narratives were divided according to the speaker's location when the disaster occurred. The differences in the situations clearly show the diversity of the experiences of these individuals as well as their emotions and rational reactions.

2.5 Review

The distinguishing feature of the Toshinroku Project is that it centers on Tohoku University. Faculty members and students currently see and talk to each other as they go about their daily lives in much the same as they did before the 3.11 disaster. However, many of them returned to the university after extraordinary experiences: some worked continuously on relief and reconstruction efforts, some were among those temporarily evacuated from their homes, and others learned about the earthquake while they were overseas. Observing this broad range of experiences, what happened to these individuals on 11 March, and what they did before returning to their lives at the university, gives a relatively clear picture of the impact of a major disaster on the university community. Recording these experiences and sharing them clarifies both the facts of the "disaster" from an inside perspective and the realities of post-disaster reconstruction in its aftermath.

This project has made us keenly aware of the immense diversity of people who gather at the university, although this is often taken for granted. Tohoku University is one of the largest national universities in Japan with internationally evaluated research achievements. The total student body numbers 16,000, with 3,000 faculty and the same number of administrative staff members. The university has 15 graduate schools, three professional graduate schools, six independent research institutes and centers, and a hospital. It is divided into five campuses. Considering also those associated with other institutions, such as the Tohoku University library, archives, and the hospital, one can begin to imagine how many students and faculty members there are at the university and the diverse fields (e.g., humanities, social sciences, natural sciences, and engineering) in which these people may work. This institutional diversity points to the different conditions under which university members, whose daily activities vary widely by discipline and profession, experience disasters.

The 3.11 disaster occurred during the university's spring break. Many students had returned home to other parts of Japan or were traveling with their fellow students to celebrate their graduation (in Japan, graduation is in March) when the earthquake struck. Other students whose homes were closer were living in the areas affected by the tsunami. After the earthquake, some students who had been evacuated from their homes stayed with relatives or friends. We wondered how the international students felt when they left Japan for their home countries or decided to continue their studies. The results show that their experiences should not be divided into broad categories of "national" or "foreign" students. There were also questions about how faculty members dealt with other concerns and worries besides reaffirming the safety of their students, such as the safety of their own children. How did the lecturers, who were abroad at the time, learn of the disaster, and what did they do until they could return to the university? All these factors involve extremely multilayered and complex processes.

Perhaps the most revealing information for the project organizers were the details of the experience of the administrative staff and employees of the companies doing business with the university. These stories did not differ much from those of faculty members and students regarding the conditions faced immediately after the disaster. After that, however, these individuals quickly responded to the situation and devoted their energy to restoring normalcy at the university. Some members of the administrative staff sent their children to live with grandparents or relatives in other parts of the country so that they could devote themselves completely to the restoration. The tasks faced by the staff of the facilities department, which was responsible for repair and restoration, were daunting. The library faced an incredible amount of work as they toiled to put scattered books back on the shelves and restore stacks and reading rooms. We probably would not have known anything about how these people felt if the project had not given them the opportunity to talk about their experiences.

Some narratives were far from the experience of white-collar workers within the university campus. The Fisheries Field Station was in Onagawa, a town that was destroyed by the tsunami. The captain of the maritime training vessel at this station is an employee of Tohoku University. Some staff members at Kawatabi University Farm in northern Miyagi prefecture specialize in raising cattle. Important stories that captured the experiences of our university colleagues include stories about the Kawatabi Farm staff's concerns for the cattle and their efforts to provide adequate feed for them as well as the captain's courageous decision to take the training ship out into the rush of the tsunami waters and into the open sea to protect it.

Unfortunately, we were unable to interview people from some parts of the university because either of their refusal of our inquiry or our failure in scheduling.[5] Prior to this project, I was not fully aware of the variety of jobs that are part of the environment in which we teach and do research nor did I realize how much the university is sustained by the efforts and sense of mission of so many people.

It is also important to consider the difference in employment status between full-time and part-time faculty and staff. Unlike the full-time faculty and staff, most university's part-time workers are employed under annual contracts with no chance of promotion. This difference has some bearing on the individual's decision to return to the profession. I distinctly recall a part-time employee whose employment contract was renewed every year, saying with a sigh of relief, "I feel very fortunate that my employment will continue despite the disaster." The university has a social mission, namely, to provide higher education and conduct research, but it is also a social institution that employs people, an aspect that I became truly aware of for the first time. The vendors of the university shop did not only provide food and necessities to those associated with the university but also to the local people near the campus. We also learned about the dedicated efforts of employees of companies doing business with the university to support the reconstruction process.

The relationship between interviewer and disaster victim in our project could be considered interchangeable because the interviewers were also survivors of the 3.11 disaster. The group session method did not establish an absolute difference between the two either. We adopted such a session format because this method would allow people to talk about their experiences and those listening to them to sometimes reverse their positions, and we hoped that this would induce a kind of healing process and sense of community among the people gathered. However, among those who acted as interviewers, some expressed hesitance at calling themselves "victims." The terms "victim" and "affected area" are both absolute and relative.

Some readers may doubt that it was worth recording the experiences of those who were not in the hard-hit areas.[6] There were indeed people at the university who suffered virtually no hardships or were unaffected by the damage, but there were others who had very painful experiences. Many people associated with the university lost their lives. It is important to note that the narrative record shows the enormous variety of experiences of survivors at the university who have tried to return to normality.

The reconstruction of local communities that have been severely affected is extremely important. Modern society is made up of many social nodes that intersect across multiple levels. A university is a place of learning and work. It is also a practical community consisting mainly of people who may live far away and come voluntarily to this place for specific purposes. In this sense, our recording project is an attempt to shed light on the facts of a society that has undergone a major disaster as a community as a typical organization in modern society. It should show how different the disaster experiences of those who formed this community were and how these individuals eventually returned to develop the community.

The memories recorded in this project generally focus on how people coped with difficulties triggered by the disaster and how they overcame them. The recollections of what happened may not have been entirely positive as they were portrayed in later accounts. These reports, therefore, are no more than a part of the disaster experience of the Tohoku University community. Although they knew about the project, I have heard that some people resisted the idea of talking about themselves and were reluctant to participate. Among the participants at the meetings, some only listened. Even among those who did talk about their disaster experiences, some refused to allow their stories to be made public because rereading their accounts was too painful. This indicates that the horror of the disaster was still fresh. It was not ethical to intrude on their emotions in the name of science. I believe the project deserved to be conducted, even though the accounts may only represent the "partial truths" (Clifford 1986), or rather, precisely because they can only present partial truths. It was only by chance that we were able to share the memories of these people; the Toshinroku Project was woven from the fabric of such memories told under the conditions described previously.

2.6 Conclusions

This study is a reflective ethnography of a project that members of the project team engaged in to record memories of the 3.11 disaster. The manuscript addresses both the process and the meaning of this endeavor. This chapter could be considered a rather subjective field diary. Still, it contains concrete and feasible options for academic action regarding what an anthropologist may face if a catastrophe strikes close to home. In other words, it is a treatise on the academic responsibility of anthropologists who may not have suffered a great personal loss but are intimately connected with a disaster.

This chapter began with how anthropologists should respond to disasters that have occurred in their hometowns. Next are some conclusions and suggestions for colleagues and other researchers in the field.

When researching regions or societies, a specialist may choose some options in the face of a disaster. One might travel to the hardest-hit areas to conduct participant observations and interviews. These data may provide insight into practical solutions for the recovery process and lead to a deeper understanding of how a given society engages in sociocultural processes when facing extreme conditions. In addition, one could invite and collaborate with other anthropologists who are researching the same region but live and work in other locations to either help with the recovery efforts or participate in the research. However, for those with a lack of local and regional knowledge but who have methodological and theoretical knowledge of anthropology, I recommend starting a recording and archiving project in their communities with the help of friends and colleagues. Many anthropologists may study cultures that are far from home. Therefore, recording and archiving represents a feasible course of action in such a situation, consistent with the academic responsibility of an anthropologist in their home society.

The participatory way in which this project was carried out, in collaboration with colleagues and friends, provided an opportunity for reflection for those involved. This type of project illuminates the unknown dimensions of the damaged community that are obscured by the hurried atmosphere of the reconstruction process. A participatory project that involves sharing empathy with/from others allows people to grasp the significance of their own experiences, even if the damage done was relatively minor. It also provides an opportunity to understand the depth of the experience of someone who may be sitting next to you.

After a huge natural hazard like those that occurred in Tohoku, many people might feel a sense of social curiosity. Inside and outside the affected area, people want to know what happened. Certainly, if one is in a position to do so, one should contribute to sharing this information with the public. On the other hand, another task of anthropologists is to document the sociocultural processes that follow a disaster in areas that are not as severely affected. The social and scientific importance of recording and archiving should not depend on the extent of the damage. We need to uncover the different behaviors and emotions of people facing disasters in all places. I suggest that the recording and archiving project at one's neighborhood or self-archiving fits into this context and would recommend it to researchers who find themselves facing a similar situation.

The main outcome of this project was to provide a picture of multidimensional suffering after a disaster. People in modern times are inevitably exposed different conditions of disaster risk because of their lifestyle and the separation of home and work. This separation results in three sociocultural dimensions: first, there is a separation between our life at home and our life at work; second, there is a distance between us and our colleagues, who also live in different areas; third, we commute between our home and our workplace, which means that we move often from one place to another. These three different processes sometimes facilitate collaboration but, at other times, provoke problems among people during the recovery process.

Notes

1 Tohoku University has five main campuses in Sendai City, Miyagi prefecture. Additionally, there are the University Farm and the Fisheries Field Station in different municipalities in the same prefecture; however, these places are 2.5-hour drive away from the city of Sendai.
2 Toshinroku is an abbreviation of TOhoku daigaku SHINsai taiken kiROKU.
3 Generally, Japanese people do not prefer to speak in a roundabout manner and avoid expressing their true feelings in public, as expressed by the term tatemae ("public face," "façade"). Additionally, many staff and students at Tohoku University underestimated the value of recounting their experiences in the face of all that needed to be done for the "real" victims affected by the tsunami.

4 Some of the statistical analysis provided here is drawn from Professor Kimura
  Toshiaki's work (Takakura and Kimura 2012, 37–42).
5 Several other projects organized by individual laboratories or departments
  have archived the disaster experiences of Tohoku University (TU 2013; TUSM
  2012) from various perspectives. One distinguished project, the "Michinoku
  Shinrokuden" project, has created an integrated online archiving system (http://
  shinrokuden.irides.tohoku.ac.jp).
6 I recommend the book, *3.11 Record of Wails*, edited by sociologist Kanabishi
  Kiyoshi (2012), in which survivors of extreme situations were asked to record
  their experiences.

3 Reflections from a survey of post-disaster intangible cultural heritage

3.1 Sciences and disaster

The exceptionally destructive Great East Japan Earthquake and the subsequent tsunami had a very strong impact in Japan and around the world. Since the earthquake, numerous scientific projects and social programs have been implemented for mental and physical health, community reconstruction, local job creation, tsunami hazard reduction, and nuclear disaster mitigation (Higuchi 2011; Irikura 2012; Minami et al. 2011; Suzuki, Y. 2012; Yamakawa 2012). The responses of anthropologists in Japan reflect various individual behaviors, including participating in volunteer work, organizing public lectures or workshops, and conducting surveys (Kimura 2016). This chapter explores the contribution of anthropologists' activism to the affected region and its communities.

I examine this question from the perspective of my personal experience, as I was also personally embedded in the post-disaster context. I was not an expert on Japan having devoted my professional interest to exploring Siberian and Northeast Asian ethnographies. However, given the difficulties faced by the region in which I was living, an acquaintance working in the cultural policies of the Miyagi municipality coincidently invited me participate in an applied research project of intangible cultural heritage at home. As a researcher, I began my anthropological projects with some hesitation because the condition of the disaster areas was immediately apparent and because of my lack of local ethnographic knowledge. I soon learned that anthropologists could contribute to the disaster recovery process in unique ways. While working as the leader of the commissioned project to survey the damage to intangible cultural heritage caused by the tsunami in Miyagi prefecture, I found that there was an overlap between the recovery needs expressed by policymakers and anthropological expertise. This is a retrospective review of the project and its considerations from an anthropological perspective. I present a case study rather than a general discussion of either

DOI: 10.4324/9781003348757-3

disaster anthropology or social engagement. Any giant disaster should be idiographic rather than nomothetic, although I believe certain findings are transferable to a much broader context through inductive reasoning.

First, I describe the project on intangible cultural heritage and the tsunami considering the Japanese context. Then I discuss its significance from the perspective of the discipline and suggest possible forms of anthropological social engagement in disasters.

3.2 Anthropologists in Japan after the catastrophe

Following the 3.11 disaster, anthropologists all over the country asked themselves how they could take part in relief efforts as citizens and how they could also contribute to the generation of specialized knowledge. For example, the Tohoku Regional Colloquium of the Japanese Society for Cultural Anthropology met on 15 May 2011 at Tohoku Gakuin University for "A Gathering about the March 11 Great Earthquake: Sharing experiences as victims and researchers." This meeting, which was attended by more than 50 anthropologists, included discussions between participants both from inside and outside the affected region and underscored sharp contrasts of opinion about the pros and cons of conducting a post-disaster survey (Hayashi et al. 2016).[1]

However, in my opinion, the tenor of the discussion at this meeting was predominantly negative, suggesting that Japanese anthropological expertise could not be used directly to address the 3.11 disaster. The same tenor can be found in anthropological publications. While saying, "I do not intend to criticize all the actions of the researchers and experts . . . who rushed into the quake-stricken areas as being either self-righteous or self-serving," one researcher warned that their surveys and research really did little to help the victims of the disaster (Suga 2013, 2). Another scholar, seeing the disaster unfolding before his eyes, wrote, "There is no field of science or methodology that can help to physically improve the situation," concluding that "all we can probably do is remain engaged on a long-term basis" (Kimura 2013, 14). Anthropology is a "slow science" (Kimura 2016) that conducts field research while maintaining a close relationship with the people in the particular area of study.

However, anthropological surveys have been conducted under difficult conditions. As can be seen from books about the 3.11 disaster published one after another in 2013, some anthropologists started extensive field research immediately after the disaster. One of them, Shōichirō Takezawa (2013, 2016), spent nearly eight months at the evacuation center in Ōtsuchi-chō, Iwate prefecture. In his book, he describes the reconstruction process from a local perspective, including residents' management of the evacuation center.

In a collection of essays, Tom Gill, a professor at a Japanese university, and his colleagues discuss the choices made by disaster-affected individuals and communities and how they grasped the situation that they were in. He examines the functions of cultural continuity in the emergency situation of a catastrophe and the emergence of innovative changes (Gill et al. 2013a, 9). Anthropologists using this approach were rather an exception at that time. Considering the many anthropologists who wanted to use their expertise in the face of an unprecedented disaster, I thought it useful to consider the somewhat-simpler survey approach and its effectiveness as an answer.

The study of disaster-affected intangible cultural heritage was conducted differently from traditional anthropological fieldwork. Moreover, as a government-commissioned project, the survey differed from a purely research project. With this in mind, readers may find it inappropriate to contrast the results of this survey with those of the studies mentioned previously. This chapter explores how, precisely because of this difference, survey projects on intangible cultural heritage can be placed in an anthropological context. The argument is made that this approach can become part of the research methodologies in the field of anthropology in disaster-stricken areas.

As a researcher working in an area affected by the earthquake, anthropologists should contribute to reconstruction policy, and the local administration, in fact, expects contributions from anthropologists. Based on this experience, public anthropology should include an option for an anthropology of disaster risk reduction.

3.3 Earthquake disaster reconstruction plan and commissioned project

Prior to the 3.11 disaster, the Agency for Cultural Affairs (Bunkacho) in Japan launched the Program for Promoting Tourism and Regional Invigoration by Making the Most of Cultural Heritage (Bunka Isan o Ikashita Kankō Shinkō/Chiiki Kasseika Jigyō). Shortly after the 3.11 disaster, the government specifically invited the three disaster-affected prefectures of Iwate, Miyagi, and Fukushima to apply to the program as a disaster policy (Kodani 2012).

Miyagi prefecture submitted the application. The prefecture organized a special committee consisting of several non-governmental organizations for promoting folk culture as well as the Cultural Properties Division. One of the projects planned by the committee was the "Survey of Intangible Cultural Heritage Affected by the Great East Japan Earthquake in Miyagi Prefecture." The project aimed to obtain data concerning the potential for the recovery of local communities with intangible cultural heritage in the tsunami-affected coastal areas of Miyagi prefecture and information about the damage to tangible cultural heritage. For example, this information included brief descriptions of intangible cultural heritage and the conditions before the disaster, including the related social organization; the death toll; the condition of local evacuation; and material losses, such as drums and costumes. The municipality government designated a list of the targeted intangible cultural heritage. The project provided data and information to help the local government make appropriate decisions about the activities of its cultural administration. This project was commissioned by the Tohoku University Center for Northeast Asian Studies, where the author works.

The organizational aspects need to be discussed to understand how this commissioned project worked. The Prefectural Cultural Properties Department, Education Planning Office, Lifelong Learning Department is an office under the Miyagi Prefectural Ministry of Education. This means that the survey project was linked to the hierarchical structure of the Prefectural Ministry of Education. Therefore, the prefectural education committee could ask the education committees at the city, township, and village levels to participate in the project.

The staff members of the commissioned project first visited the city, town, or village board of education in the district to which they were assigned when they conducted the first round of the survey. These municipal boards of education supervise information about intangible cultural heritage in their local areas, especially information about societies for preserving *kagura* (a type of Shinto theatrical dance) and other folk performing arts. At the prefecture's request, local authorities provided researchers with this information. In most cases, the first informants were representatives of these associations. Having obtained information from them, researchers could easily find interviewees, as in an ordinary anthropological investigation. The existence of such an organizational system was a great blessing, as contacts with specific informants were able to be secured before researchers arrived in the particular target area for the survey. This was an advantage for the city, town, and village boards of education because even in the initial stages of the field survey, they were able to know what kind of people would enter and conduct the surveys and in what way. A network of connections was built with the cultural preservation associations, the municipal boards of education offices, and the prefecture to resolve difficulties, such as the possibility that a person who agreed to be interviewed might later sue. In addition, researchers had also decided in advance that, as a rule, more than one survey staff member would visit a target area to inspect the houses and temporary shelters where victims were housed. In cases where confidence in the interviewers had been established after several visits, one staff member was allowed to come alone.

The survey was conducted from November 2011 to March 2013. The survey organization consisted of 22 researchers (survey officers) and about ten graduate students in the city of Sendai City (auxiliary survey officers). The survey officers were assigned to the districts for which they were responsible. When conducting the survey, they were usually paired with a student as an assistant. Municipal school boards introduced the researchers to intangible cultural heritage preservation associations; survey officers then went into the field to conduct the survey. Each survey was assigned to a district to ensure continuity in successive phases of the survey. Each survey lasted one to two days, and over a period of one and a half years, the survey officer typically visited the assigned district six to eight times, although the actual number of days varied depending on the survey officer. The primary method of collecting information was by interview, but if an event was held, the survey officer could also collect information as a participant.

This method resulted in uniform documentation of oral interview responses, which were noted, collected, and sorted by district. Survey officers conducted the surveys over a period of 152 days. The interviews with approximately 120 people (257 times in total) resulted in 1,000 pages interviews, ethnographic documentation translated into English, and 250 photographs. What was unique about this survey project was the introduction of a methodical survey system and the collection of a huge amount of formal records both in books (Takakura and Takizawa 2014) and on websites.[2]

3.4 Salvage in disaster and anthropology

In the understanding of the research team, this was a disaster salvage anthropology project. The essence of the project was to document threatened cultural heritage. The local government was concerned it could disappear; therefore, cultural rescue is a perfect description of the project. However, there was another requirement: the documentation of the local intangible cultural heritage should contribute to the future development of the local community.

After the 3.11 disaster, salvage projects became popular in Japan. Many institutes, organizations, and even individuals have tried to dig up memories and organize recordings of the disaster (Shibayama and Boret 2019). Owing to the development of information technology, such as social media, vast amounts of fragmented information, images, and sounds have accumulated and circulated on both organizational and personal sites on the Internet. National and local newspapers, individual journalists, and many local not-for-profit and non-governmental organizations published survivors' narratives and local photographs from before and after the disaster (Takakura and Boret 2021). Some institutions, such as libraries and universities, have launched participatory video interviewing projects in which they rent video cameras to citizens to record the narratives of family members and friends.[3] Everyone involved thought it necessary to record the effects of the catastrophe. Forgetting was a sin, and salvage was good for their memory. A contracted project fits this pattern; the local government entrusted this duty as part of a social trend.

However, anthropologists need to discuss why salvage is required and ask what kinds of contributions could be possible for academics in these social contexts. The reason for this lies in the history of the discipline. The word "salvage" carries a special meaning in the anthropological context. Postmodern criticism has made it impossible to reproduce the notion of the anthropological subject as an "other" that exists in a time that does not coincide with ours (Fabian 1983). Does "salvation" denote the "eternal primitive culture?" (Shimizu 1992) Therefore, we must first consider the reasons for "salvation" in the context of anthropological knowledge.

Three anthropologists offer stimulating ideas on this subject. The first opinion is that of the American anthropologist Jacob W. Gruber (1970), who claims that ethnographic rescue is one of the foundations of anthropology:

> Salvage provided the opportunity for human contact and human contrast. . . . we feel that in the disappearance of the savage, in the irrevocable erosion of the human, we inevitably lose something of our own identity.
>
> (Gruber 1970, 1298)

Most contemporary anthropologists criticize the idea of "the disappearance of the savage" because the word "savage" is discriminatory and it means the people without history from the ethnocentric view. However, what happens if we replace "the people" as a neutral term with "the consequences of catastrophe?" Certainly, the survivor of the catastrophe rebuilds something in a certain way, but it is also true that some things and some people are lost forever. Recognizing and recording what was lost is a typical act of salvage, which opens up an encounter between people based on differences. In a disaster setting, a sense of loss should be treated appropriately to facilitate people's quest for something related to their recovery. This is the essence of cultural salvation. Remember that many anthropologists in Japan have been reluctant to conduct field research in areas severely affected by the 3.11 disaster. Those who did not act may have lost the chance for human contact and sense of human contrast to make anthropological contributions.

The accumulation and use of data on human differences beginning in the 18th century shaped the forms of systematic explanation that would later constitute anthropological theory (Gruber 1970, 1289–1290). Gruber also states that any science should have a unique "organization of the particular kind of information" as a methodology and "system of explanation" as a theory. The accumulation and use of data on human differences from the 18th century onwards shaped the forms of systematic explanation that would come to constitute anthropological theory (Gruber 1970, 1289–1290). This implies the possibility of gathering data other than according to the canon. Certainly, the method of intensive participant observation properly and accurately focuses on human differences and universals, but other methods can also provide data in different ways. The sense of disappearance or loss justifies salvation, which opens their perspectives on human differences and cultural diversity. This is convincing logic in the context of disasters.

The idea of rescue or "disappearance" may remind us of colonial anthropology. The negative history of that discipline's treatment of exploited people is undeniable. On the other hand, rescue and "disappearance" can be invoked in other fields such as visual research. Margaret Mead in her article titled "Visual anthropology in a discipline of words" formulated her thoughts on this topic as follows:

> The recognition that forms of human behavior still extant will inevitably disappear has been part of our whole scientific and humanistic heritage . . . because these are disappearing types of behavior, we need to preserve them in forms that will not only permit the descendants to repossess their cultural heritage, but that will also give our understanding of human history and human potentialities a reliable, reproducible, re-analyzable corpus . . . [which] can never be replicated in laboratory settings.
>
> (Mead 1995, 3, 8, and 10)

Mead defends the importance of photography and film as a research method. The "rescue" is justified without any hesitation, precisely because it is assumed that every cultural behavior and concept is not "eternal" but instead is constantly changing. We must find something that deserves to be a record against oblivion, contributing to our search for "human potentials." After a disaster, the "potentials" could be community resilience, which is the collective ability of a neighborhood to deal with stressors and efficiently resume the rhythm of daily life through cooperation following an event (Aldrich and Meyer 2014, 255). In terms of visual anthropology, at this moment in history, we sit both at the site of fieldwork and at home in front of our digital technology terminal, which now enables the encounter that is our "decisive moment," to use photographer Henri Cartier-Bresson's famous phrase (Imahashi 2008). We always come to the crossroads to save something that has disappeared.

Koester and Niglas have recently discussed the role and value of the visual salvage ethnography in the context of Siberian studies. For the Itelmen, the indigenous people of Kamchatka, filmmaking as a part of ethnographic practice contributes not only to the recording of culture but also sensitive and powerful measures against the trends of cultural loss. Koester and Niglas claimed that, "Salvage anthropology in the 21st century is enriched by adding this sensorial, individualizing, and inherently temporizing dimension to the documentation processes" (Koester and Niglas 2011, 58). For the Itelmen, filmmaking as part of ethnographic practice contributes to the recording of culture and acts as sensitive and effective action against the trends of cultural loss.

Salvage does not always contribute to the construction of an "eternal primitive culture" but, rather, opens up new encounters with human potential, which in turn can contribute to sociocultural revitalization, especially in disaster situations. This supports the claim that salvage anthropology deserves to be organized as an option for applied anthropology during disasters.

3.5 The context of policy tasks

Anthropological fieldwork is often more concerned with identifying tasks than testing hypotheses. This feature makes it possible to apply analysis methods to various societal and cultural spheres, which is normally an advantage; however, in times of disaster, it is perceived as a problem. To further illustrate this point, disciplines such as urban planning, civil engineering, and clinical psychology are explicitly delineated areas of study; thus, it is easy to conduct surveys as part of supporting research in disaster areas. In comparison, anthropology has surprisingly few areas of unique expertise. Anthropology is characterized by its ability to put the views of existing disciplines into perspective or provide alternative frames of reference. However, these features of anthropological expertise have proven detrimental to researchers in this regard. Utilizing expertise in supporting disasters recovery requires that the areas of research prescribed within the discipline.

In this context, the intangible cultural heritage project was carried out on the condition that it was tied directly to regional rehabilitation in an institutional way, reaffirming the importance of passing on popular and traditional culture. Anthropological expertise in disaster relief was sought in the disaster recovery support field to assist in government-designated areas of intangible cultural heritage. This facilitated access to survey sites. Ethical issues related to conducting surveys in disaster-affected areas were resolved to some extent through this system of government outsourcing. In practice, when the survey began, participants generally understood why there was no open opposition to its objectives.

A skeptical anthropologist might doubt that intangible cultural heritage, such as folk performing arts, can truly contribute to the reconstruction of a local community. The reality that needs to be highlighted here is that the three prefectures of Iwate, Miyagi, and Fukushima have all acknowledged such a contribution in their post-earthquake reconstruction plans. The governmental agency for cultural affairs organized and funded the special program of cultural heritage immediately after the catastrophe (Takakura and Takizawa 2014, 296). Therefore, this project should be examined in light of this important premise.

From the standpoint of Miyagi prefectural government policy,[4] engaging in the survey project meant carrying out a "project to support the restoration of intangible cultural heritage" as a specific recovery effort within the administrative category of "rebuilding the local community." The policy categories at the same level in the disaster recovery plan were "supporting victims' way of life," "securing housing for victims," and "ensuring a safe living environment." Specific recovery efforts included "financial loans to support the disaster," "building social housing to restore infrastructure," and "promoting earthquake-resistant structures." This arrangement places the revival of intangible cultural heritage on the same level, within the political structure, as the resettlement of people.

However, the inclusion of intangible cultural heritage at this level does not mean that it enjoys the same priority from a political perspective. The promotion of earthquake-resistant buildings has a much higher priority in terms of the budget size and the social impact of construction in the near future. However, the important point to consider here is not the size of the budget but that policy issues exist in the government's recovery plan, to which fields like anthropology can make positive contributions.

Local governments do not conduct surveys or research. Therefore, disciplines such as anthropology, folklore, and sociology are considered to be specialties related to intangible cultural heritage management. A system is in place to outsource studies to researchers in these fields. Another important point is the government's expectation of short-term engagement and the scholarships' results. This is the opposite of anthropological fieldwork, which involves building long-term relationships with local communities.

In this context of administrative reconstruction, the question of delimiting the object of research must be reconsidered. As a former leading Japanese anthropologist, Tamotsu Aoki, once argued, it may be true that "studying anything from any angle" is a strength of the discipline (Asahishinbun 1995, 10); however, this statement appears undeniably naive when one considers what this discipline can do in the face of an earthquake compared with what can be accomplished by the more "practical sciences." Therefore, the Japanese government needed to draw on the expertise of anthropology to preserve intangible cultural heritage as part of its reconstruction policy. The expertise of anthropology in the field of intangible cultural heritage was considered necessary for the reconstruction effort by both society and the government immediately after the disaster. In Japan, the applicability of anthropological expertise and its ability to meet social needs has been largely associated with development issues, ethno-regional conflicts, and refugee issues in developing countries. It is important to recognize that intangible cultural heritage is only one area in the context of the 3.11 disaster.

We need to show where anthropology's strengths lie. Various disciplines collaborate in a disaster-affected area. In this context, the areas that can be handled by anthropology are defined by its past accomplishments and its social impact. It needs to be understood that anthropology is not championing the ability to research absolutely anything but that the discipline has special spheres in which it can meet societal needs.

3.6 Breaking away from the long-term participant observation method?

Some anthropologists may feel antipathy toward such a project because they are close to the government with the applied orientation. The author understands the dismissive attitude toward surveys and relief projects in normal times. However, such attitudes seem extremely nihilistic in the wake of disasters. When a government asked for academic input on disaster policy, anthropologists, like all academics, tried to find a way. The prevailing premise in managing reconstruction after the 3.11 disaster is that intangible cultural heritage can contribute to the rebuilding of local communities. In support of this premise, anthropologists should use their specialized expertise to become more involved in society. They need to ask under what types of conditions intangible cultural heritage can be useful for rebuilding local communities. Conversely, under what types of conditions is the revitalization of intangible cultural heritage not useful? Trying to answer these questions is essential for anthropologists in the field of post-disaster reconstruction policy.

To some extent, antipathy may be related to the methods of participatory long-term observation in anthropology. As mentioned earlier, it is not easy, either ethically or logistically, for researchers to go into an area affected by a disaster. However, we must not forget that the method of long-term participant observation is nothing more than an "ideal" method. In the normal process of doctoral studies in social anthropology, we have conducted long-term participant observation. However, do we continue with such studies on the same scale after entering the academic world? Were one to continue with the same study village, it may well be possible that this could be achieved. However, in many cases, subsequent studies are conducted using the comparative method or over larger areas, in a manner that does not rely solely on long-term participant observation. The survey naturally included some participant observations. Still, it was based more on written records of oral recollections drawn from interviews conducted over a relatively short time. This was an inter-organizational survey. The appropriateness of surveys based on this method should be examined more closely. First, a disaster relief project requires that a relatively short-term survey be conducted as quickly as possible. Having personally conducted this survey, I have come to believe that, at a minimum, an emergency survey to assess the affected intangible cultural heritage in the aftermath of a disaster is somewhat effective and socially useful.

3.7 Discussion

In the aftermath of a major disaster in which a regional community has suffered immeasurable damage, a viable option for professional anthropologists is to collaborate with local heritage management organizations to improve local heritage management. Such an approach could well be a framework anchored in Japanese society that defines the government's expectations about anthropologists and their relationships with the government based on the historical development of anthropology in Japan. There must be different organizational structures in different regions and with different types of government. However, it is our knowledge of the culture and fieldwork methods that determine the expectations of non-anthropologists for the contribution of anthropology, and these are the same in all countries and regions. After the 3.11 disaster, an important lesson for anthropologists is to find ways to apply our expertise in a new situation. This is the only path that anthropologists can take; however, it should be emphasized that in the post-3.11 disaster world and in response to the question posed to anthropologists about how we should deal with disasters, the revival of intangible cultural heritage as a means of social recovery requires us to think deeply about methods, theories, and organizations.

This survey project should be conducted in the first phase of the government's disaster recovery plan, the recovery phase. In every disaster, there is an initial phase for recovery activities. These were the conditions for the project, which required a specific method and, in the case of Japan, the implementation of a collaboration between anthropologists and the government. In a different context, the collaboration might have involved a different kind of organization and different kinds of authorities. In other words, there is still the possibility of various aid projects or pure research projects to be conducted in the regeneration and development phase. The famous Japanese human geographer and anthropologist who conducted research on the post-1933 Sanriku tsunami disaster, Yaichirō Yamaguchi (2011), began his research about three years after the devastating tsunami. His topic was the reason why people return to areas prone to tsunamis. This topic and his survey methods still give us clues. The beginning of a survey is significant in disaster research, and each post-disaster period raises its own questions and requires survey methods that are appropriate for addressing them.

UNESCO regards intangible cultural heritage as an important factor in maintaining cultural diversity in the face of globalization. Intangible cultural heritage is believed to promote intercultural dialogue and strengthen mutual respect for other ways of life. In this project, it became clear that intangible cultural heritage contributed to building the resilience of the community. However, this is not unique to Japan. The project was embedded in the Japanese social context. One could organize this kind of work in collaboration with non-governmental and non-profit organizations in other contexts as well. In the case of Hurricane Katrina in 2005 in the USA, for example, American folklorist Carl Lindahl organized a project in which survivors conducted interviews among themselves (Lindahl 2007). Les Field and Richard Fox (2009) discuss the practical social value of anthropological knowledge and argue for the importance of collaboration and co-theorizing in ethnographic research. Collaboration should be the foundation of the ethnographic process, from project conception to fieldwork to writing. Many stakeholders should conduct disaster salvage anthropology: anthropologists, the government, non-governmental organizations, and the affected people.

Regardless of differences in the local contexts, anthropology for salvaging local intangible cultural heritage through comprehensive and short-term surveys provides an effective and socially valued applied research response to disasters. Therefore, it must be emphasized that anthropologists must be prepared to organize research teams capable of conducting a systematic emergency survey of disaster-affected intangible cultural heritage at any time, both in a different research region and in the region where the anthropologist lives and works. This should be done as part of a disaster risk reduction policy.

Notes

1 In 2011, other significant meetings included an open lecture on "The Great East Japan Earthquake as Witnessed by a Folklorist" (Tohoku University), held on 25

June 2011 under the auspices of the Folklore Society of Tohoku; the 206th regular meeting of the Chubu Anthropology Colloquium, held on 23 July 2011, to discuss "Anthropology in Crisis Part I, Anthropology's Role in Disaster: Lessons from the Great East Japan Earthquake" (held at Sugiyama Jogakuen University); and the 860th meeting of the Folklore Society of Japan, held on 3 December 2011, "Memories and Accounts of the Earthquake Disaster: Toward Rebirth of Folklore" (Tohoku University).

2 Accessed 19 February 2022. http://mukeidb.cneas.tohoku.ac.jp/.
3 To grasp the development of related salvage projects, I recommend non-Japanese readers review the Japan 2011 Disasters Archive managed by Harvard University Reischauer Institute of Japanese Studies (http://jdarchive.org/en/). The Michinoku Shinrokuden – Tohoku University Archiving Project (http://shinrokuden.irides.tohoku.ac.jp), written in Japanese, is one of most comprehensive databases of the projects.
4 Accessed 19 February 2022. www.pref.miyagi.jp/site/ej-earthquake/fukkou-keikaku.html.

4 The structural time in the folk performing arts

4.1 Disaster mitigation and culture

The relationship between disasters and intangible cultural heritage might be similar or different from the relationship between disasters and tangible cultural heritage. UNESCO defines intangible cultural heritage as traditions or living expressions inherited through generations, such as the performing arts, festive events, and rituals (UNESCO 2018, 5). This definition has four features: tradition or contemporary setting, inclusiveness, representativeness, and community involvement.[1] Natural hazards destroy tangible artifacts and monuments; they also strike people, places, and communities related to intangible cultural heritage and disrupt knowledge, skills, and technology. In this context, we must prepare against the impact of disasters on both intangible and tangible cultural heritage. On the other hand, combining living heritage with people, places, and communities could lead to an alternative way of thinking about how intangible cultural heritage might mitigate the effects of disasters because the "loss [of intangible cultural heritage] can be generative, facilitating the formation of new values and attachments" (Littlejohn 2021, 1).

The role of culture in disaster mitigation and risk reduction is a result of recent disaster policies. The United Nations Office for Disaster Risk Reduction (UNDRR) encourages strengthening communities' capacity to manage disasters and risk reduction (Hyogo Framework) (Oxley 2013) and advocates disaster risk reduction through integrated and inclusive economic, legal, structural, health, and cultural measures, among others (Sendai Framework) (Morris and Ueyama 2020). What are the cultural measures for disaster risk reduction, and how does intangible cultural heritage contribute to disaster mitigation? These are the core questions addressed in this chapter.

One of the salient features of the post-3.11 disaster recovery was the role of intangible cultural heritage, in particular, the coverage and anthropological

DOI: 10.4324/9781003348757-4

focus on local performing arts and festival events as symbols of the community's recovery (Kimura 2016; Takizawa 2019). The geography of small coastal communities with historical traditions and the mourning-related religious function of the performing arts were among the reasons for focusing on these aspects. The survivors had the opportunity to commemorate the victims and reflect on the future through these heritage activities in local settings. In the context of disaster recovery, the government and private companies financially supported these events. According to anthropologist Isao Hayashi (2012), people who suffered from the tsunami and were living in evacuation housing acted in folk performing arts for victims' souls several months after the catastrophe on a particular prescribed date after their funerals, which were conducted in the local Buddhist way. Iizuka (2021) and Lahournat (2016) recognize the effects of intangible cultural heritage on survivors' psychological recovery and its integrative quality, which contributes to identity and community formation while promoting ties with locals and non-locals, including disaster volunteers.

Sociologist Kyoko Ueda posed an insightful question, "Why do those affected by the Great Earthquake conduct traditional events under the emergent conditions?" (Ueda 2013, 43). She argues that the answer is that the rituals provide the concept of repetitive time to people who have to deal with practicalities in an irreversible timeline provided by the reconstruction policy, thus encouraging people to return to their daily lives. In addition, rituals have an integrative function, which serves to bond individuals to society (Michell 1996). Rituals that are part of intangible cultural heritage have two functions, namely, the evocation of a sense of routine and social integration, both of which contribute to the recovery of post-disaster society.

Here, the focus is on the local religious rituals of Shintoism, which include local performing arts like *kagura* or *shishimai* and some related festivals. The argument put forth is about the function of rituals in cultural heritage in the post-disaster setting. Questions of how a ritual can contribute to disaster reconstruction after the Fukushima nuclear accident and why people conduct local performing arts and festivals are addressed. Furthermore, the questions asked are how can anthropologists contribute to the cultural policy on disaster reconstruction? How can we propose the idea of a better management for this type of intangible cultural heritage to policymakers?

4.2 The difficulties after the Fukushima disaster

Much anthropological research has been conducted on the effects of the disaster following the explosions at the Fukushima Daiichi Nuclear Power Plant after the Great East Japan Earthquake. These studies argue the local perception of risk of radioactivity and examine how it damages social reliance and local identity (Gill 2013; Ikeda 2013; Iwagaki et al. 2017; McNeil 2013; Uchiyamada 2017; Yamaguchi 2016). Some studies have focused on mother-child evacuation (Horikawa 2016; Morioka 2013; Oikawa 2018; Tatsumi 2014) in the context of distrust toward the government and science, which in turn damages the cohesion of the family, kin, and the local community. The government decided the levels of safety in terms of radiation based on what they considered "scientific" knowledge, but the members of a family often could not accept this decision. In particular, mothers who had infants or young children were more sensitive to the effects of nuclear radiation on their children.

Tatsumi (2014) described how mother-child evacuees risked isolation from their families and local communities. Due to different evaluations of the risk of radiation for father and mother and the conditions of employment among family members, mothers and children were often evacuated separately from their husbands in areas further from the Fukushima Daiichi Nuclear Power Plant. The behavior of those mothers sometimes provoked criticism toward them from those who had already accepted (believed) governmental judgments on safety. The explosion at the Fukushima Daiichi Nuclear Power Plant affected social reliance in the family and the local community.

How can this phenomenon be explained theoretically? The main reason is the health risk perception of nuclear radiation, which could be called "biological citizenship," a key idea of Adriana Petryna's Chernobyl anthropological studies. Biological citizenship is "a massive demand for, but selective access to, a form of social welfare based on scientific and legal criteria that both acknowledge injury and compensate for it" (Petryna 2016, 37). Petryna describes the predicament of those affected by the Chernobyl disaster while arguing that biological citizenship is key to the building of civil society, in opposition to the socialist regime (Petryna 1995). On the other hand, in the Fukushima disaster, biological citizenship brings about the destruction of social ties for family and kinship by disabling social consent in anticipation of the future. Sociologist Ulrich Beck states that "poverty is hierarchic, while smog is democratic" in the contemporary risk society (Beck 1998, 50). Poverty is distributed and forms social classes; therefore, class struggle is an important solution against poverty. On the other hand, democratic smog or radiation rather nullifies the traditional type of solidarity against risk.

Let us combine the predicaments of the Fukushima disaster with the role of rituals in disaster recovery. The question to be addressed is how rituals, with their evocation of a sense of routine, and the function of social integration work to restore damaged social ties and community reliance in Fukushima. In other words, should anthropologists propose policy recommendations for disaster recovery, emphasize the role of rituals that are part of intangible cultural heritage, and explain how these activities can restore damaged solidarity in the affected communities? One concern is whether research on ritual activities may discourage mothers from evacuating from areas affected by the Fukushima disaster because the emphasis on these intangible cultural heritage rituals may act as pressure for social integration for those who may be hesitant to evacuate. The following section provides an ethnographical description of two cases of intangible cultural heritage ritual activities and examines their effects on the disaster recovery process. Finally, the possibility of policy recommendations in terms of intangible cultural heritage ritual activities in post-disaster conditions are considered.

4.3 Two cases of intangible cultural heritage

4.3.1 Case 1

The first case involved local performing arts and *shishimai* dance in mid-August, which is a part of a ritual that is conducted every four years at the Suwajinja Shinto Shrine in Shimoniida coastal village in Iwaki City (Figure 4.1). The origin of this ritual dates back to the 17th century (1634). Dancers in three different types of deer-styled masks perform the dance to honor the local Shinto gods and ask for a rich harvest and offspring prosperity. Approximately 20 men performed the opening dance with miniature

Figure 4.1 Group picture of the Shimoniida *shishimai* dance (August 2015)
Source: Hiroki Takakura

wooden phalluses before the deer mask dance. The dance groups and a band with the Japanese flute first dedicated the dances to the Shinto shrine and then paraded through the village streets during the daytime.[2]

The youth-men association (*seinenkai*) and the executive member of the *ujiko*, the patrons or caretakers of the local shrine, play leading roles in organization and management. The *ujiko* organization is deeply related to the village's history. Officers are elected from each street association (*tonarigumi*) every four years. Street associations are neighborhood organizations for mutual collaboration on funerals and landscaping, which date back to the era of the Tokugawa Shogunate. The members of the youth-men association come from these street associations. Two weeks before the ritual, they began preparing the necessary tools and training. These men gathered at the youth-men association house every evening after work, even on weekdays.

Shimoniida village, where this ritual is held, is located in Iwaki City approximately 35 km from the Fukushima Daiichi Nuclear Power Plant. This area was categorized as a "safe zone" by the Japanese government. Therefore, some people had evacuated to Iwaki City from regions close to Fukushima Daiichi, which were now classified as "restricted residence zones" or "difficult zones to return to." On the other hand, some people had evacuated from Iwaki City and relocated to other regions. Despite the tsunami damage and consequent radioactivity issues, the local communities decided to organize their festivals because they wanted to conduct them as usual, although there was some disagreement. Most residents believed that the implementation of the festival contributed to commemoration and recovery.

During fieldwork, the level of the activity of local social organizations was very surprising. The youth-men association has an extraordinary role in the integration of community members. The association also implemented a well-organized collaboration with senior citizen executives, who were Shinto parishioners. The phallus representation as an extraordinary open expression of sexual behavior was notable. This *shishimai* dance is a typical ritual that provides people with a sense of *communitas*, or the liminal phase in the rites of passage.

4.3.2 Case 2

The second case concerns the *Nagareyama* dance in the town of Futaba during the annual summer festival (Figure 4.2), which is organized by the Futaba Women's Association. In this dance, women wear Samurai costumes and sing local ballads. According to the local history, the dance was originally a male performance; however, women participated in the performance

Figure 4.2 Snapshot of *Nagareyama* dance (January 2016)
Source: Hiroki Takakura

even in the 1960s (Fukishima ken 1964, 1001–1005). The community, located 5 km away from the nuclear power plant, is categorized as a "difficult zone to return to"; thus, even in 2021, the level of danger was still high. Residents of Futaba are now spread across different locations in Japan.

When the nuclear accident occurred, Futaba residents evacuated from their homes; one of the places residents went was Tsukuba City, 160 km south of Fukushima Daiichi. Here, Emiko Wakamura (pseudonym), a leader of the local women's association, initiated the ballad dance activity because the association wanted to organize a show to thank Tsukuba's citizens for their hospitality. The community members had settled in various places; therefore, Wakamura needed to reorganize the dance group. First, she needed to organize a class to teach the dance and prepare special costumes. Due to a shortage of participants, some men joined the dance groups after the disaster. Wakamura's activity functioned as a meeting node for those living in different places.

Did this activity help members of the dance group restore their ordinary sense of everyday life before the nuclear accident? When the dance was performed, former residents imagined life before the disaster and associated this with the tragedy of the evacuation and the fact that it was difficult to return home. On the other hand, when the interview with Wakamura continued, an interesting historical background was discovered. According to her, this ballad dance was originally a special program of the annual summer festival of *Soma-Nomaoi*, which is a nationally known Shinto festival, including Samurai costumed horse racing and a flag-scramble competition. The main organizer of the festival was the *ujiko* organization, the patrons of the local shrine for Soma City's citizens. The members of the Futaba Women's Association participated in performing the *Nagareyama* dance at the *Soma-Nomaoi* festival along with groups from six other neighboring communities. Approximately 80 women from Futaba Town participated in the *Soma-Nomaoi* festival. The dance group in each community had the chance to participate in *Soma-Nomaoi* every six years because of the rotation of these six locations. In addition, the local group performed their dance during the annual summer festival in each community. The reason for the participation of the six local communities in the *Soma-Nomaoi* festival lies in their regional history. These rural communities administratively belonged to Soma City during the Tokugawa Shogunate period (17th to 19th centuries). The maintenance of the *Nagareyama* dance recognizes the regional historical legacy from the Samurai period and the feudal domain once governed by the Soma clan (Figure 4.3).

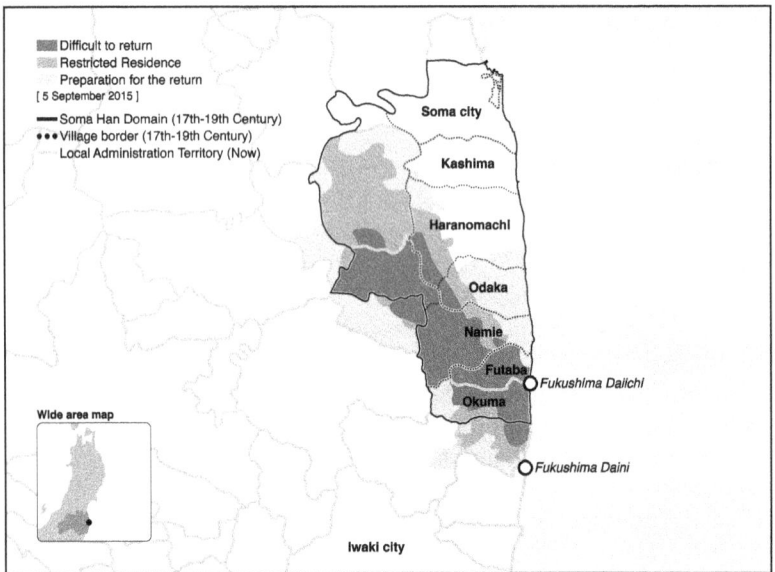

Figure 4.3 Historical-Cultural Legacy of Social Organization in Fukushima Coast and the Evacuation Zone from Fukushima Daiichi Power Plant

Source: Hiroki Takakura

4.4 The Nuer and Fukushima: two concepts of time in intangible cultural heritage

This section considers the role of rituals in disaster recovery and further explores the interpretation of the cases described previously to introduce the familiar anthropological concept of "time" stated in the canonical African ethnography of the Nuer by E.E. Evans-Pritchard. He described two different time concepts. The first is "ecological time," a reflection on the Nuer's relations to their environment: "It appears to be, and is, cyclical . . . the daily timepiece is based on the round of pastoral tasks . . . such as milking, driving of the adult herd to pasture" (Evans-Pritchard 1969, 95). The second is "structural time," a reflection on the interaction between social groups:

> [T]he Nuer has another way to roughly state when events took place . . . by reference to the age-set system. The distance between events is reckoned in terms of structural distance, which is the relationship between groups of people. It is therefore entirely relative to the social structure.
>
> (Evans-Pritchard 1969, 105)

How can we consider the theoretical implications of the Nuer's conception of time in understanding the Fukushima case? First, we could easily identify the concept of ecological time in both cases. In the case of Fukushima, the cyclical nature, which is a feature of the ecological time, can be seen in allowing people to experience a rhythm of life similar to that before the nuclear disaster, as has been already noted in previous studies on the role of rituals in post-disaster settings.

However, it is important to emphasize the elements of structural time seen in the two cases. The collaboration between the young men's association, the street associations, and *ujiko* organization of Shinto patrons in the *shishimai* dance every four years and the collaboration of six local communities participating in the *Nagareyama* dance groups in a six-year rotation should be emphasized. Both rituals were considered in terms of structural distance, the relationship between the groups participating in the events in different years. The participants certainly felt some unfamiliar emotions, which were uncovered when they joined these dances. They were able to understand the historical-geographical relationships between the communities, which now had become difficult to distinguish. The ritual provided participants with a sense of structured historical-cultural depth embedded in everyday life; it establishes a sense of "here and now" among people and also awakens the possibility of alternative, multifaceted relationships between people.

The structural time in rituals provides a new form of social integration, which goes beyond the "here and now" and may be critical in repairing damaged solidarity or in supporting mothers and children who have evacuated due to the radiation risks.

I would like to consider the political implications of this ritual type of intangible cultural heritage for the evacuees. Both the *shishimai* and the *Nagareyama* dance provide a perception of routine and social relationships while simultaneously demonstrating alternative time-space concepts and potential for new ways of communication. Rituals do not always force people to affirm the context of a given community. Rather, they can renew the social structure to some extent. In particular, the practice of the *Nagareyama* dance is a trial both for recovering the once-existing historical structure represented by the livelihood of the residents of Futaba and for renewing the social relations between the evacuees.

In a post-disaster society, rituals highlight the structured legacy of human life, which is the historical-geographical basis of everyday life. If one considers the power of rituals that are part of intangible cultural heritage in terms of their contribution to innovations in social structures, it is important to place them at the forefront of future development in a revised form of social organization.

4.5 Conclusions

The core question of this chapter was how cultural traditions can confer a sense of recovery in people. While the features of the disaster surrounding the Fukushima nuclear accident are described, we also examine how rituals, as part of intangible cultural heritage, work in post-disaster societies. One conclusion is that intangible cultural heritage rituals have a new role in disaster recovery. Previous studies point to the evocation of a sense of routine and social integration as crucial to recovery, a phenomenon that is almost identical to the ecological time concept of the Nuer. This chapter uncovers the structural time concept in the Nuer and the historical-geographical depth of rituals, which may renew previous ways of social integration and attachment.

Another conclusion of this study relates to policy recommendations from anthropologists concerning the advantage of the structural time in rituals that are part of intangible cultural heritage. If we consider the role of culture in post-disaster settings, it should contain not only traditional activities but also modern festivals. Anthropologists should encourage intangible cultural heritage rituals either in customary or contemporary settings because the structural time concept enforces the diverse forms of social attachment and value. In addition, voluntary leadership based on ritual traditions is key to local initiatives in disaster recovery. Intangible cultural heritage rituals with structural time may become effective social instruments for disaster mitigation under certain conditions.

Notes

1 Accessed 14 February 2022. https://ich.unesco.org/en/what-is-intangible-heritage-00003.
2 The ethnographic film of this *shishimai* edited by the author is available at the following website: http://hdl.handle.net/10097/63692.

5 The strategies of the paddy farmers with indigenous knowledge

5.1 Indigenous knowledge and disaster

The purpose of this chapter is to uncover the cultural processes underlying local methods of agricultural reconstruction in the Tohoku region of Japan, which was ravaged by the 3.11 disaster. In particular, focusing on the case of farmers in Miyagi prefecture, the effects of the tsunami on local rice fields, and how local knowledge contributed to agricultural reconstruction are examined. The role of local knowledge in post-disaster reconstruction and how its application has bolstered the resilience of farming communities in these areas is discussed.

Disasters provide a rare opportunity to observe resistance, and resilience in a society sometimes reveal the essence of the social mechanisms in a given community (Hoffman and Oliver-Smith 2002). Anthropologists regard disasters as processes that can expose vulnerability in sociocultural systems. Their approach seeks out aspects of the social process rather than investigating the particulars of an event. In the case of the 3.11 disaster, some descriptive anthropological studies have discussed the roles of cultural continuity in terms of identity and morals (Gill 2015; Gill et al. 2015) and festivals and rituals (Kimura 2016; Takizawa 2014), while others have focused on resilience and the indigenous knowledge embedded in coastal fishing communities (Wilhelm and Delaney 2015; Ueda and Torigoe 2012).

Indigenous knowledge has also been discussed in disaster risk reduction research (Marin 2010; Hayashi 2012; Oliver-Smith 2013b; Speranza et al. 2010). These studies are not purely theoretical and have been recommended by United Nations agencies and other international organizations as useful references. Triggered primarily by the Sumatra-Andaman earthquake and Indian Ocean tsunami in 2004, this area of research further involves interdisciplinary contexts and policy orientations. Since the catastrophe, international policymakers and academics have paid increasing attention to indigenous knowledge (e.g., local oral traditions concerning disasters)

DOI: 10.4324/9781003348757-5

as effective educational resources for risk reduction. The UNDRR actively advocates for indigenous awareness and local knowledge as efficient tools for disaster risk reduction, both in the pre-disaster (prevention) and post-disaster (recovery) phases. Modern science might be skeptical of any relationship between indigenous knowledge and disaster risk reduction; however, some indigenous knowledge is specifically related to disasters and this type of knowledge is culture specific. Hence, researchers in this field investigate local knowledge related to risk reduction and consider its applicability beyond the culture in which it emerged (Shaw et al. 2008, v–vii).

Several researchers have explored these issues. One examined how the traditional housing culture contributed in the reconstruction policy after the catastrophe (Pasupleti 2013). Another categorized local and indigenous knowledge related to disasters to identify knowledge that could be scientifically tested and that was relevant for disaster risk reduction (Hiwasaki et al. 2014). These works contributed to the adoption of the document issued by the 2015 UN World Conference on Disaster Risk Reduction, which recommended ensuring "the use of traditional, indigenous, and local knowledge and practices" for disaster risk reduction to "complement scientific knowledge in disaster risk management" (UNISDR 2015, 15).

In this chapter, indigenous or local knowledge in disaster risk reduction research is used, rejecting any dichotomy between science and local-indigenous knowledge. Previous anthropological research has criticized the idea of people "immobilized by their belonging to a place," "groups in remote parts of the world," or "prisoners of their 'mode of thought'" (Appadurai 1988, 37 and 39). The indigenous knowledge referred to here is collective, centered on a given community, related to a particular geographical area, transmitted both by insiders and outsiders, and inclusive of science and technology, with individual differences among communities. Within these parameters, the role of local and indigenous knowledge on post-disaster agricultural recovery processes is explored. As indigenous or local knowledge is not fixed, the dynamics and complexities of local knowledge are analyzed, and how local knowledge works in the disaster reconstruction process is examined. This involves closely examining the interaction between local knowledge, post-disaster reconstruction policies, and related science and technology and discussing how this process can lead to greater resilience in farming communities. "Resilience" refers to individual or group capacities to deal with disasters and to resist and recover from their effects (Oliver-Smith 2009, 14). It encourages "the researcher to bridge the 'shear zone' between (dynamic) adaptation and (static) resistance" (Alexander 2013, 2714). The core research task of this chapter is to uncover the complexities of local agricultural knowledge. While explaining the social and cultural constraints and particularities to rice cultivation, in particular the creation of various work schedules depending on choices of agricultural methods, the mode of agricultural recovery is examined. Focusing on the case of paddy field farmers in the southern part of Miyagi prefecture, agricultural knowledge related to post-disaster risk reduction is identified in order to explore its applicability to other areas.

5.2 The tsunami in Yamamoto Township

The tsunami caused more than 85% of the deaths in the 3.11 disaster.[1] The giant tidal waves that swept the coastal regions resulted in a massive death toll. In the immediate aftermath of the waves, the rice paddies were covered with a large amount of debris piled up by sediment accumulation and exacerbated by further damage from the tsunami. The farming population dropped precipitously due to a combination of causes: the death toll, the loss of agricultural machinery, and damage to the farmland. During the years that passed after the tsunami, the government and local administrations worked on reconstruction. Most farmlands had been restored for possible cultivation; however, the farming population had not recovered to anything near pre-tsunami levels. The reasons for this are the loss of farmers by death or migration after the disaster and the aging of the farming population. The Japanese government has instituted measures to support and aid agricultural organizations, helping them (groups or individuals) to expand their cultivated land. The goal is to enhance labor efficiency so that fewer farmers can successfully cultivate relatively larger areas of land. This effort may solve some agricultural recovery and restoration issues, many of which were thorny policy issues, even before the disaster. The tsunami exposed the weakness of the sociocultural system in Japanese agriculture.

My anthropological field research for this chapter was carried out from 2011 to 2015 in Yamamoto Township, which is located in the southern-most coastal part of Miyagi prefecture, adjacent to Fukushima prefecture (Figure 5.1). Before the Tsunami, the population was 16,704. Yamamoto is a rural area whose economy relies mostly on the agricultural and fishing industries. The town is known for its strawberries, apples, and Hokki sea clams (Sakhalin surf clam). However, rice is the most important agricultural product. Although the net income from rice production is relatively low, 72% of Yamamoto's agricultural land comprises paddy fields, and rice cultivation is the basis of the local farming industry. Farmers whose main products are strawberries or vegetables usually cultivate rice, beyond self-consumption needs (Yamamoto 2018a).

The 3.11 disaster earthquake and tsunami struck the long, low coastline, sweeping away homes and businesses in the Yamamoto community and flooding 80% of farmland. The flooded area extended over 24,000,000

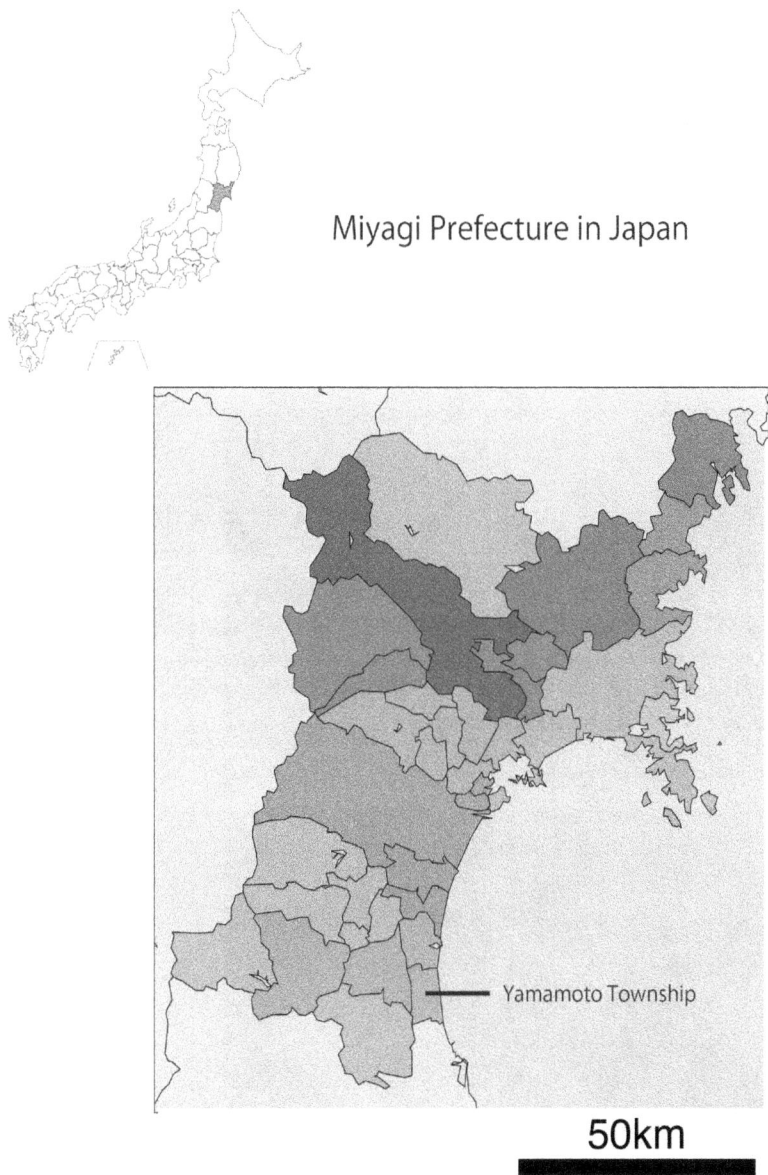

Miyagi Prefecture in Japan

Yamamoto Township

50km

Figure 5.1 Map of the research field

Source: Lincun

Yamamoto Township
before the tsunami
10 December 2009

Yamamoto Township
after the tsunami
6 April 2011

Yamamoto Township
at the present
1 June 2015

Figure 5.2 Before and after the tsunami in Yamamoto Township
Source: Google Earth

square meters (2,400 hectares) – 37.2% of the total area of the township (Figure 5.2). The disaster-affected area included 2,913 households and a population of 8,990 people, almost half of whom were in the town at the time of the disaster. In total, 636 people were killed and 3,302 houses were destroyed or severely damaged.[2] The 1,440 hectares of paddy fields recorded in 2010 were reduced to 657 hectares in March 2011, a loss of approximately 54%. The loss ratio of vegetable fields and agricultural garden land was 23% (Table 5.1). The damage to rice production has been a complex and severe problem, exacerbated by changing demographics and Yamamoto's complicated structure of property ownership.[3]

In Miyagi prefecture, the number of farmers decreased by 15.7% between 2010 and 2015. In 2015, farmers aged over 65 were 59.7% of the total. In terms of management, subsistence farmers (a legal category indicating those who cultivate rice only for self-consumption) controlled 24.8% of the agricultural land, and their average plot was less than 0.3 hectares. Farmers who produced rice for commercial sale used 74.6% of the land; the land size was less than 1 hectare for 30%, between 1 and 3 hectares for 33%, between 3 and 5 hectares for 7%, and more than 5 hectares for 4.6% of commercial producers.[4] A notable feature of this distribution is the aggregation of small-scale plots, regardless of whether they are cultivated by subsistence- or market-oriented farmers.

In 2014, the Yamamoto local government announced a rice production reconstruction policy to be implemented over several years. One element of this plan was land consolidation. The administration intervened specifically to encourage absent landowners to lease their land to active or large-scale farmers.[5]

5.3 Rice and Japan

The anthropological literature on rice farming in Japan is copious and can be roughly classified into four categories. The first three represent the conventional research trends. One is related to the study of the anthropology of Japan, in which rice farming is seen as a cornerstone of culture and identity

Table 5.1 The agricultural recovery policy plan for Yamamoto Township in 2013

	2010	2011	2018 (estimate)
Population	16,704	14,628	13,700
Agricultural land	2,016 ha (31.7%)	1,122 ha (17.4%)	2,034 ha (31.5%)
Paddy field	1,440 ha	657 ha	1,432 ha
Field and garden	606 ha	465 ha	602 ha

Source: Yamamotocho 2013

(Embree 2010; Befu 1971; Ohnuki-Tierney 1993). The second is exploring the cultural history of rice farming in Japan using comparative perspectives from East and South Asian rural regions, focusing on rituals and world-views (Yanagida 1969; Sugiyama 1967). The third category is the documentation of traditional knowledge and technology that prevailed before mechanization (Hayakawa 1973; Takeuchi 1976; Ogawa 1997). The last category centers on contemporary perspectives on rice production. These studies describe the function of environmental conservation and the inevitable sociocultural changes brought about by the use of new technology (Ishimoto 2014; Yasumuro 2012; Watanabe 2011).

Among these approaches, the third type suggests a methodology that can identify, classify, and prioritize local knowledge related to rice farming and evaluate the possible role of this knowledge in the post-disaster setting. Previous research (e.g., Takeuchi 1976; Hayakawa 1973) proposed three phases in the cultivation process of rice: (a) sowing-planting, (b) growth management and weeding, and (c) harvesting. Takeuchi (1976, 28–32) noted that the threshing phase was primarily mechanized by the early 20th century, and the mechanization of planting and the use of chemical fertilizer and weed killers did not begin until the 1950s. This chapter focuses on the local knowledge related to these three phases of rice production.

The site of field research was decided by accident. As discussed in Chapter 3, I undertook the commissioned salvage project in Miyagi. As a leader, I organized several anthropologists and graduate students as a team and sent them to some villages in the Miyagi coastal region. The southern villages of Yamamoto Township were randomly included in my designated survey region, and the government asked us to study the local *kagura* dance and other performing arts associated with Shinto shrines. While surveying the damage caused by the tsunami to the local cultural heritage, I recognized other serious issues affecting the livelihood of the people working in agriculture in the area. This was the point of departure of the research project described here.

When starting this project on agricultural disaster and adaptation, several specialists at the local agricultural cooperative and the agricultural technology development agency of the local government were interviewed. Then the fieldwork method was adopted and focused, individual on-site interviews were used. This approach involved repeated interviews with selected respondents at the site of their activities, namely, in the paddy fields during each phase of the work. This method seemed preferable than the typical participant observation because of both physical and ethical difficulties. Most individuals affected by the earthquake and tsunami still lived in temporary housing, and it was difficult to make room for an anthropologist to stay in the immediate area.

To explore the cultural dimensions of adaptation, two target farmers became the focus. Before the earthquake, these individuals engaged in small-scale farming as a side job on land inherited from relatives. Post-3.11 disaster, they are both classified as mid- or large-scale farmers. Each of them was visited more than 40 times between 2011 and 2015, covering all three phases of the work calendar plus the winter preparation for cultivation.

The first farmer, Mr. Takahashi (pseudonym, born in 1945), lived in the coastal area of Yamamoto. He lost his house, agricultural machinery, and five family members. While many farmers quit rice production, he expanded his cultivated paddy fields from 3 hectares to 30 hectares after the tsunami. The second farmer, Mr. Adachi (pseudonym, born in 1943), lived in the mountainous part of the township; thus, his property suffered relatively little damage. He had previously cultivated 1.5 hectares of his ancestral plot, increasing to 3.5 hectares after the tsunami.

When the government implemented the plan to promote large-scale agriculture, some farmers, including my informants, increased the area under cultivation because they took over land abandoned by other farmers. The physical condition of paddy fields and plot sizes were the same as before. These farmers resulted to work in more paddy field plots, devoting the same amount of labor to them as before the earthquake. Figure 5.3 shows one of Mr. Takahashi's cultivated agricultural land maps, illustrating each plot and user as of 2014. The initial "T" in the plot means that Mr. Takahashi cultivates it. Table 5.2 shows the rice farmers according to the plot as numbered in Figure 5.3, pre- and post-tsunami. There was a decrease in the number of farmers from 15 to six. According to the local government, 70% of farmers had restarted cultivation in 2014. If the increased acreage were spread over a single large field, the use of machinery would be effective and easy. However, the Japanese farmers in general cultivate their own plots of land even though they are relatively small (Ohizumu 2014), which prevents the efficiency of machinery. In the next section, we examine how farmers have adapted to this complexity and the role of local knowledge about rice cultivation.

5.4 Traditions and innovations

Before examining the role of local knowledge in the aftermath of the disaster, we will briefly look at some developments in rice production, including a review traditional practice before the 1950s. Two critical technological innovations concerning seed rice prior to the disaster, a method of managing seed rice and the advent of highly engineered seed rice, are essential to understanding farmers' adaptations after the tsunami.

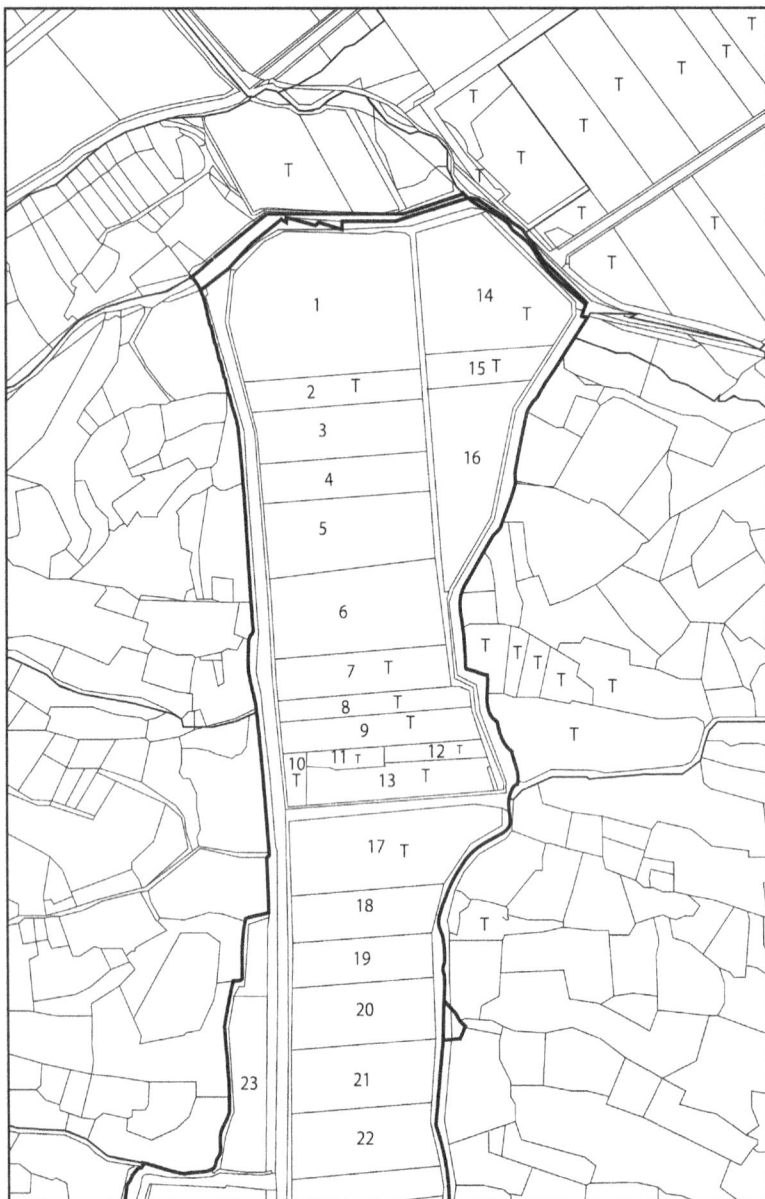

Figure 5.3 Agricultural plots in a part of Yamamoto Township in 2014
Source: Hiroki Takakura

Table 5.2 Property relationships and users in Yamamoto Township before and after the tsunami

Plot number	User before tsunami		User after tsunami
(in the Figure 5.3)			
1	A	→	D
	A	→	D
2	B	→	T
3	C	→	C
4	B	→	Q
5	D	→	D
6	E	→	P
7	F	→	T
8	G	→	T
9	G	→	T
10	H	→	T
11	H	→	T
12	H	→	T
13	H	→	T
	H	→	T
14	I	→	T
15	J	→	T
16	D	→	D
17	K	→	T
18	L	→	D
19	D	→	D
20	M	→	P
21	M	→	P
22	N	→	D
23	O	→	O
	15 persons		six persons

Japanese farmers followed practices that evolved over a long period and prevailed until recently, propagating their original seed rice passed down through ancestral family lines, which resulted in the actual biological diversity of rice. This practice enhanced the identity of the family line (Ohnuki-Tierney 1993, 29 and 181). The tradition has gradually disappeared since the 1970s and is now almost extinct in this region. Increasingly rigorous quality-control requirements for rice prompted by market demands have made it more difficult for farmers to achieve a substantial market share for their seed rice. Since the 1970s, Japanese consumers have become accustomed to buying rice with brand names, such as Sasanishiki or Koshihikari, which people perceive as having especially good quality and flavour. In 1978, Miyagi prefecture began promoting intensive seed rice production, centered in one region, and started to sell breed-controlled seed rice to farmers through the local agricultural cooperative. Today, most rice farmers in Miyagi buy these types of seed rice. They are not hybrids but are controlled products of the original seed rice.

Traditionally, there are three types of seed rice distinguished by when they come into ear: *wase*, earlier (growth speed) ear; *nakate*, middle ear; and *okute*, later ear (Table 5.3). These expressions refer to types of rice and stages of childhood development: *wase* also means "precocious child," while *okute* means "late bloomer." Farmers in Yamamoto can buy nine types of "brand" seed rice. According to the local people, Kirara is the sole *wase* or early ear, which comes into ear around 15–20 July. The five brands of the middle ear are Tsuyahime, Hitomebore, Sasanishiki, Manamusume, and Mochigome. They usually come into ear between July and 10 August. The three brands of the latter ear are Koshihikari, Kaguyahime, and Mirukī kuīn (Milky Queen). These come into ear later, around 13–15 August, coinciding with the Bon festival, when annual Buddhist rituals related to honoring ancestors occur. Each of these brands of seed rice has a unique taste and a slightly different coming-into-ear period, even those in the same general categories of *wase*, *nakate*, and *okute*. The selection of seed rice is a critical decision for farmers, who must consider the critical variables of the market value, weather, and labor availability.

Table 5.3 Three traditional types of rice seed

	Term	Explanation	Average period of the coming into ear after the rice planting*	Informants' explanation of the date of the coming into ear	Commodity information from the informants
1	Wase	Earlier growth speed type	50 days	July 15–20	Kirara
2	Nakate	Middle growth speed type	60–70 days	between July and August 10	Tsuyahime, Hitomebore, Sasanishiki, Manamusume, and Mochigome
3	Okute	Late growth speed type	80 days	later than August 13–15	Koshihikari, Kaguyahime, and Mirukī kuīn (Milky Queen)

Source: Author's field notes and *www.kubota.co.jp/kubotatanbo/rice/management/ear-emergence.html

Purchasing seed rice is similar to futures trading. Farmers order seed rice in 5 kg units because the seed rice production depends on these orders. If the ordering period were February, deliveries would occur in March the following year. The order cannot be revised or cancelled. Mr. Adachi described this process as follows:

> When I order seed rice, I need to decide what to get by predicting the weather for the year. In this region, we often have years without a definite end to the rainy season. Therefore, we are always worried about whether we should plant a *wase* or *okute*. For example, Koshihikari, a type of later ear, is resistant to cold. It is important not only to choose the right type of seed rice but also to decide when it should be sown. This affects my labor calendar.
>
> (Interview, 24 July 2014)

Farmers in Miyagi choose one or several types among the nine varieties, considering labor conditions and business strategies. Decisions are based on both market value and growth characteristics; each farmer makes decisions based on what will fit their individual conditions.

The second pre-disaster technological innovation is engineered rice; seed rice is coated in a substance containing iron powder, making the seeds heavy enough to be sowed directly on paddy fields (Yamauchi 2012). In the process known as *taue*, or rice transplantation, Japanese farmers first sprout unhulled seed rice using the conventional method and then lay the sprouted seeds in separate nursery beds. When the sprouts become seedlings, they transplant the seedlings to the paddy field, filled with a shallow layer of water. Planting seed rice directly in a field without a layer of water is called *chokuha*, which is a new technology that originated in California rice production in the United States. The seeds are planted in the ground, germinate, and grow into seedlings, then water is flooded into the field. Because of the weight of the iron coating on the seed, the seed rice does not drift when the field is flooded and takes root in the soil. There are two ways to conduct *chokuha* direct seeding, either by a helicopter or a seeding machine. Helicopter seeding can be performed quickly, making it possible to sow an extended agricultural plot efficiently. Seeding machines take more time, but they sow the rice seeds in lines, which afford greater harvest yields than plots planted by helicopter.

5.5 Local knowledge in post-disaster adaptations

How have local farmers restarted rice production after the disaster? The focus of this study is on farmers who have been expanding their cultivation without an increase in available labor. Here, the role of local knowledge in implementing adaptive methods according to each process of sowing/planting, growth management/weeding, and harvesting is demonstrated.

5.5.1 Choices made in sowing and planting

The farmers interviewed had adopted the *chokuha* direct seeding technique for their land after the disaster. However, they only partially adopted it. When asked, Mr. Takahashi explained his reasoning:

> The reason for the mixture of the direct-planting and rice-transplanting methods is the different harvest periods that result from the two cultivation methods. When one uses the rice transplanting method, it is possible to reap the rice from the beginning of October, while using the direct method, reaping usually begins around October 20. Using both, a single farmer can stagger the labor time required for an extended plot. There is certainly another way to distribute labor time, based on using a type of seed rice that has its own period of reaping. When farmers plant these seeds, they plan on different reaping periods, considering the timing and labor required. However, in terms of market sales, this method poses difficulties for the following reasons. After reaping, the next process is threshing using a machine. Japanese consumers are very sensitive to the distinctions among varieties of rice, and it is impossible to sell rice mixtures. Each type of rice must be threshed separately, so it does not mix with other types. Farmers usually have their own machines; thus, when they thresh a different type of rice, they must clean the machine thoroughly, which is very labor intensive.
>
> (Interview, 4 July 2014)

In 2014, Mr. Takahashi planted three types of seed rice and used two planting methods. Figure 5.4 shows his paddy field on 4 July 2014. The photographs show four different types of seed rice/planting methods, all separated in his cultivated fields. The first is Tsuyahime seed rice planted by the seedling-transplantation method; the second is Manamusume seed rice using the transplantation method. However, for Hitomebore seed rice, which is the seed rice for his major production, Mr. Takahashi used direct seeding and transplantation methods in separate fields.

The idea of farm scheduling – managing agricultural timing either by the planting method or type of seed rice – is not a recent agro-technological development. Mr. Adachi explained two methods of rice seedbed (*nawashiro*) used in preparation for rice transplanting. These methods were employed even before the mechanization of agriculture in the 1960s and

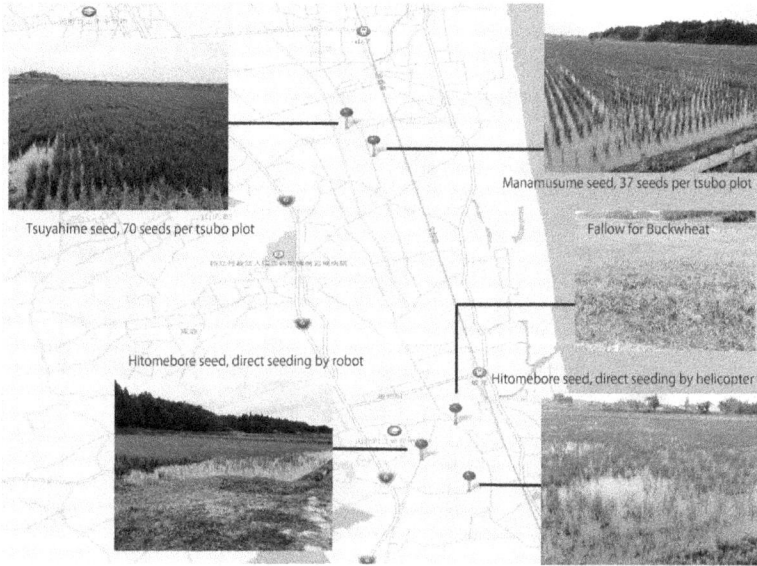

Figure 5.4 Various paddy field conditions managed by a farmer on 4 July 2014

Source: Hiroki Takakura

allow farmers to organize time shifts for viable work schedules. In the *mizunawashiro* method, which is considered archaic, seed rice is planted in dedicated nursery plots of paddy fields saturated with water. In the *ho'onsetchū* (-*nawashiro*) method, farmers plant seed rice directly in dedicated plots with soil in paddy fields and, then, cover the seedlings with plastic sheets or oiled paper. This method was invented in the 1930s. The seedlings grow until they are 10–15 cm in height, and then they are planted in paddy fields. The *ho'onsetchū* method is two weeks shorter than the *mizunawashiro* method. According to Mr. Adachi, because of labor limitations, the ability to manage time in this way was crucial before the introduction of rice-transplanting machines in the 1960s (interview, 24 July 2014).

After transplanting, farmers must confirm whether the young plants are firmly rooted in the paddy field. Figure 5.5 shows rice plants from paddy fields managed by Mr. Adachi. The pictures are of young plants showing roots of two colors three days after planting. Plants with white roots were transplanted from the nursery bed, and those with brown roots grew from seeds planted directly in paddy fields. When young shoots have roots with these two colors, rice transplanting has been successful. The directly planted ones are also successful.

Figure 5.5 Two colors of rice seedling roots (21 May 2015)
Source: Hiroki Takakura

Another choice concerns the amount of seed rice planted per plot, measured by *tsubo*, a Japanese unit of area equal to approximately 3.3 square meters. Planting more seeds per *tsubo* increases the cost of purchasing seed rice. The effects of this choice are physically apparent in the width of the space between seedlings in a paddy field created by automated rice-transplanting machines. Figure 5.6 shows three different widths: when farmers plant 70 seeds per *tsubo*, the space between the rows will be 9 cm wide two months after transplanting; for 40 seeds per *tsubo*, it would be 14 cm; for 37 seeds, it was 20 cm. Most of the farmers in the Yamamoto area plant 70 seeds, the amount recommended by the local agricultural cooperative.

Even so, both of my informants chose to grow fewer plants per *tsubo*. Mr. Adachi plants 40 seeds, and Mr. Takahashi, 37 seeds. They are susceptible to the cost of seed rice. Mr. Takahashi explains his reasoning as follows:

> I chose to plant 37 seeds this time, which was a challenge. Here, most farmers plant 60 seeds or more. Planting 37 seeds is an exception to standard practice and reflects a choice that will inevitably lead to a smaller harvest. The greater the number of seeds, the greater is the

70 seeds - 9 cm in width
between seedlings

40 seeds - 14 cm in width
between seedlings

37 seeds - 20 cm in width
between seedlings

Figure 5.6 The different widths of seed rows per *tsubo*, varied by the number of seeds planted (24 July 2014)

Source: Hiroki Takakura

harvest. This certainly points to the drawbacks of planting a smaller number of seeds. However, there are merits such as lower costs and good growth conditions for the seedlings. If one plants a small number of seeds, the space between seedlings is wider; therefore, growth is faster, and the seedlings grow thicker. Based on the final results, the harvest can be expected to be not much smaller than that of 70-seed planting. The wider space also helps to prevent disease in rice.

(Interview, 4 July 2014)

Mr. Takahashi learned these are things from experience. He concluded that planting a comparatively small number of seeds per *tsubo* was better than planting a larger number. In addition to the issues noted previously, planting 70 plants per *tsubo* in a paddy field creates competitive conditions among seedlings severe enough to require a significant increase in the amount of fertilizer that must be applied to ensure that the seedlings grow tall enough (interview, 25 August 2014).

The farmer's choice of seed number might appear to be related to the mechanization of rice transplanting. This choice is also grounded in traditional technology. Anthropologist John. F. Embree provided an interesting ethnographic description of rice transplanting and the role of fieldworkers as linemen before World War II:

It [*taue* rice-transplanting] is hard work, but the work is social. Ten or fifteen young men and women lined up across a field. As two linemen lay down a guide line with beads every five inches, the human line bends over rapidly, sticks seedlings into the mud, then stands up, and steps back; the lineman shouts Hai!, moves the string over five inches, and the human line bends over and pops in the seedlings. The monotonous work is relieved by constant chattering [that is] often ribald.

(Embree 2010, 99–100)

In the traditional setting, the linemen, as leaders of social labor, determined the amount of space between seedlings. A present-day farmer using mechanized rice transplanting can select the width by themselves. This kind of mechanization is an efficient reflection of traditional techniques.

Before the earthquake and tsunami, neither farmer decided to use multiple methods of sowing and planting because their paddy field plots were very small. They chose Hitomebore seed rice, and they used the rice-transplanting method, keeping the seed numbers per *tsubo* recommended by the local agricultural cooperative. Although many farmers abandoned paddy field cultivation after the disaster, others chose to cultivate more land in response to the efforts of the local government to support the recovery of rice production and facilitate the consolidation of land-use rights. These farmers manage larger paddy fields while facing a labor shortage. Local knowledge of sowing and planting contributes to their efforts to adapt to the new conditions by making their work calendar less intensive and increasing labor efficiency.

5.5.2 Basic skills of growth management and weeding

After rice transplanting, farmers must pay attention to the tillers, a lateral shoot that emerges from the base of a rice stem, that emerge from the seedlings. As the rice plant grows, the number of tillers growing from the roots increases to 15 to 20 per plant. Later, the tillers become stalks. Farmers control the amount of water in paddy fields to ensure strong and healthy tillers, which are the basis for growing rice plants that will not topple, even as harvesttime nears. Farmers temporarily drain water from paddy fields to stop tiller growth. Figure 5.7 shows this process. According to Mr. Takahashi, temporary draining of water affects rice plant growth in the following ways:

> Young stalks grow longer in paddy fields with deep water. Because submerged stalks are not comfortable in water, they try to grow faster. This lengthens the length of the stalk between the nodes. When rice stalks grow in such a way, they may topple as they continue to grow before the autumn harvest.
>
> (Interview, 9 July 2015)

Farmers consider stalks with a shorter length between the nodes in their lower parts to be resilient against wind and rain. Thus, they carefully control the water level in paddy fields and sometimes drain the fields. Each plot of paddy field connects to the irrigation channel; farmers can control the amount of water running into each plot.

Another important aspect of growth management is predicting the development of rice ears, the part of the plant that forms the rice grains. Local farmers observe the top leaves of plants from the end of July to early August. If the leaves are bent, the ear forms. The farmers call this *tomeha*, indicating that a plant has a different color. The bending of the leaves is caused by the weight of the ears. Although the sowing of seeds or transplanting of seedlings begins on the same day for each field, the appearance of ears may vary slightly within the field (see Figure 5.8). After the first signs of *tomeha* bending in some plants, it usually takes five days to occur in all plants in a paddy plot (interview with Mr. Adachi, 5 August 2014).

↑ Draining the water in a paddy field

← Rice tiller

Figure 5.7 Ceasing growth of rice tillers by cutting the water supply (9 July 2015)
Source: Hiroki Takakura

Tomeha

Pre-mature ear inside tomeha

Figure 5.8 Local concepts for the judgment of rice ears (5 August 2014)
Source: Hiroki Takakura

The stage at which all the ears of the plants in a paddy field are bent is known as *hosoroi*. Figure 5.9 shows a rice paddy during *hosoroi*. During this period, the young yellow-green ears appear to be in full bloom between the leaves, indicating pollination. When farmers confirm that paddy is in *hosoroi*, they feel a sense of relief and look forward to the harvest.

June to August is the main weeding period. Farmers usually use weed killers, although they often need to cut weeds by machine in some places. Weeding is nothing but continuous hard labor. Farmers know when they must weed by how the rice plants respond to weed growth. According to Mr. Adachi, the height of the stalks in a plot should ideally be equal; it is aesthetically pleasing and beneficial for growth management. Farmers pay particular attention to the ridges surrounding the paddy fields, which are more difficult to weed than other parts of the field. When weeds on the ridges are not sufficiently cut, adjacent rice plants are shaded by the weeds, which stimulates the rice to grow taller and results in disproportionate heights of rice in the paddy. The farmers dislike tall stalks because they are more vulnerable to damage by wind and rain. This kind of local knowledge does not directly help farmers adapt to post-disaster conditions, but it is fundamental knowledge needed to understand the maturation of rice.

5.5.3 Harvesting

How do farmers establish the best time for harvesting (*minoiri*)? Generally, the degree of rice maturity can be roughly gauged by sight, but this is not sufficient to determine the exact timing of the harvest. Farmers calculate the appropriate time by focusing on the color of the stalk, known as *shiko*, bearing the rice ear (Figure 5.10). When the *shiko* turns the same yellow color as the ear, the rice is mature. As the rice matures, the tip of the ear turns from green to yellow, and then the yellow color moves further down the stalk. This process takes several weeks. According to Mr. Adachi, rice with *shiko*, as shown in Figure 5.10, will take 20 more days to reach full maturity. This knowledge allows farmers to estimate the time of maturity for each type of rice. The rice is ready to harvest when the yellow-colored shiko comprises approximately 70% of the paddy field. The local farmers share this knowledge. The judgment to decide the harvest timing is important because if farmers wait until 100% of the plants reach this stage, some will be too mature. Their grains will have lines in the middle, and they will crack when polished in a machine. "All the rice in a paddy field does not simultaneously mature, so the point is to recognize the optimal time to maximize the volume of harvest" (interview with Mr. Adachi, 29 August 2015). Local knowledge of *shikos* is critical for the best possible estimate in planning the harvest schedule.

A rice ear in hosoroi – pollination period

Rice ears in full bloom in a paddy field

Figure 5.9 Hosoroi or pollination period (5 August 2014)
Source: Hiroki Takakura

Figure 5.10 Shiko in rice (29 August 2014)
Source: Hiroki Takakura

Japanese farmers as well as the farmers and gardeners in different cultures are known to be sensitive to the aesthetics of their fields. They prefer paddy fields with neat lines of stalks of the same height. A farmer's ability to organize an aesthetically pleasing paddy field is considered socially valuable to the community (Watanabe 2005). Yamamoto Township confirms this tendency. The farmers care about whether the growth process creates a fully crafted rice field in the last stages before harvest. They carefully note how sunlight affects the growth of rice plants and the maturity of rice ears. Figure 5.11 compares maturity levels in one plot of a paddy field on 31 August 2014. The upper photo shows healthy maturity, as most of the spike tips that have received sufficient sunlight are sufficiently bent, while the stems in the lower photo suffer from insufficient sunlight. The latter is near a bank that provides shade. Farmers carefully monitor their rice fields daily to detect slight differences in the growth of the stalks. They are also sensitive to the effects of fertilizer; the amount used affects the strength of the rice stalks. When more fertilizer is applied, the stalks grow taller, which often results in typically weak "back and legs (ashi-koshi)" of the rice that can easily be toppled by wind and rain. The ideal stalks were low and wide. However, even when farmers recognize bad conditions and cannot alleviate

Good maturity

Bad maturity due to less sunshine

Figure 5.11 Sunlight and plant growth in the same paddy field plot (31 August 2015)
Source: Hiroki Takakura

growth problems during that year, the experience adds to the knowledge for the following years' cultivation.

The farmers' choice of seed rice, the method of planting, and the number of seeds per plot (in rice transplanting) create various and delicate differences in harvest timing. This is apparent in the color of the paddy field. Although fields may appear homogeneous throughout much of the growing season, each paddy plot simultaneously displays a different color gradation from light green to yellow. Figure 5.12 shows the results of the farmers' choices. The yellow-and-green fields show that the front light-green field was planted with Tsuyahime seed rice, having a late type of middle ear. The yellow back field was planted with Hitomebore seed rice, an earlier type of middle ear. According to Mr. Adachi, his neighbor, who owns the back plot, planted rice seedlings two days earlier than he did in his front plot. As a result, on 26 September 2014, the front plot had another two weeks until harvest, whereas the back plot was ready for reaping. If these farmers had chosen the *chokuha* direct seeding, the harvest would have been further delayed. These two farmers' complex choices of seed rice and dates of seedling transplantation produced more than ten days of difference in the timing of the harvest.

While local knowledge of harvesting also does not contribute directly to the farmer's ability to adapt to post-disaster conditions, adaptive activities,

Figure 5.12 Different colors of paddy fields (26 September 2014)

Source: Hiroki Takakura

such as seed rice choices and planting methods, result in different periods of harvesting and color gradations in the paddy field. Farmers' knowledge of harvesting enables them to recognize exactly when to harvest in paddy fields with different types of rice and planting methods.

5.6 Collective and individual types of indigenous knowledge

This chapter examines the many effects of farmers' local knowledge on rice production, from selecting rice seeds to decisions about planting to growth management and harvesting. While farmers may be able to calculate differences in the rate of growth, either by their choice of seed rice or planting methods, they can also carefully foresee the growth process and recognize different growth conditions in the field. One cannot help noting that farmers speak of the ideal shapes of rice grains and rice plants in human terms (e.g., back, legs, etc.). Shorter and wider stalks are resilient to heavy rain and wind. Such ideal plants are "rice with a strong (lower) back and legs." Knowledge clusters surrounding rice cultivation can be summarized in terms of manipulating labor timing. Rice plants grow through photosynthesis and biological responses to natural conditions, including precipitation, temperature, sunlight, soil, and wind. Farmers use local knowledge to create differences in timing of rice growth to maximize labor efficiency.

Theoretically, farmers in Yamamoto Township can create 45 different work schedules depending on their choices of agricultural methods. First, there are five patterns of rice planting. There are mainly two planting methods: *chokuha* direct seeding and *taue* seedling transplantation. For the former, there are two methods: seeding using a planting machine or helicopter. Among the latter, there are three options for the number of seeds planted, namely 37, 40, and 70 per *tsubo* of the plot. Farmers choose among nine types of seed rice from three categories of growth: *wase*, *nakate*, and *okute*. These all add up to 45 options, each of which could generate a slightly different growth process in any given plot.

It is important to note the land-use structure of Yamamoto Township. Thousands of tiny paddy fields with complex property relationships exist. Each farmer needs to consider the most appropriate way of sowing, growth management, and harvesting while considering their labor capacity. In the post-disaster circumstances, the disaster recovery policy encouraged some farmers to increase the amount of land they cultivated. However, the conditions of the plots themselves remained as they were before the disaster. In other words, they remain highly segmented.[6] Farmers need to find the most efficient methods to pursue their businesses in a region with limited labor availability. This leads to the concept of time manipulation as local agricultural knowledge. Farmers have had such knowledge for a long time, but its importance, especially regarding sowing and planting, has increased since the disaster.

5.7 Knowledge in practice

How do paddy field farmers use their agricultural local knowledge to adapt to the post-disaster conditions? First, I examine the dynamics and complexities of local knowledge to show how they are applied to the disaster reconstruction process. Local knowledge of rice production can be classified into three categories: (1) maturation process, (2) environmental knowledge, and (3) biological response (see Table 5.4). Knowledge of the maturation process relates to the form of the concept and is embodied in terms expressed in the local dialect, such as *tomeha, hosoroi, and minoiri.* This knowledge is fundamental to recognize and describe the rice growth process. It also acts as a medium for communication among local farmers. Farmers exchange information on rice growth and harvest using these terms with dates or amounts of fertilizer.

Environmental knowledge refers to the relationships between soil, water supply, sunlight, and the time frame available for rice production. This is prescriptive knowledge with a descriptive form related to the physical condition of rice growth. Examples from this research include the effects of water supply on stems (growth management) and the effects of sunlight on the harvesting process. In addition, local farmers recognize the potential difference in harvests depending on whether crops are grown in sandy soil on the coast or in inland clay soil. This knowledge is common among local people and allows them to roughly estimate an agricultural plot's harvest capacity. These two types of knowledge, environmental conditions and maturation processes, are collective and traditional.

Table 5.4 Three systemized types of local knowledge

Type of knowledge	Feature	
Mature process: tomeha, hosoroi, shiko, etc.	Conceptual, communicative	Collective, traditional
Environmental condition: soil, water supply, sunshine, etc.	Descriptive, prescriptive	
Biological response: sowing type, roots number, weeding, and fertilizer	Conditional, human-plant relationship	Individualistic, innovative

Finally, biological response knowledge relates to human-plant interactions and is often expressed in conditional verbs and statements of anticipated results. We can see this in farmers' comments that if one took a particular action in the paddy field or some environmental event happened, a particular outcome would have resulted. Examples include the choice of rice seed type, decisions to use direct sowing or seedling transplantation, and the calculation of the number of seeds in a plot. Knowledge of weeding and fertilizer effects also belong to this category. All human behavior affects the plant growth and vice versa. Each farmer has a different view of certain actions and methods. The more skilled farmers are, the more knowledge they have. Importantly, this type of knowledge is individualistic and innovative. Farmers always need to adjust their methods and technological innovations to respond to different climate, soil, or economic conditions.

The local administration provided new production technologies and new land ownership regulations as part of the post-disaster reconstruction policy. The success of a farmer's adaptation to post-disaster conditions depends on the extent to which they engage with the three types of knowledge. The first two types, knowledge of the maturing process and environmental knowledge, tend to be traditional and collective in the community. However, the innovation and differentiated experience of knowledge about biological responses could lead to critical adaptations of farmers to new circumstances. Farmers can learn about the maturation process, gain environmental knowledge from their families and communities, and develop individual biological responses.

5.8 Toward a policy recommendation

This chapter focused on the role of local knowledge related to rice production since the 3.11 disaster. It shows the complex and dynamic structure of this knowledge and demonstrates that it has both traditional and contemporary dimensions. Local knowledge of paddy fields consists of indigenous wisdom passed down through several generations; however, it also contains flexible and adaptive aspects that enable farmers to cope with unknown difficulties. It is collective and allows for individual differences that make continual renewal possible.

Local knowledge can be characterized as enabling the manipulation of time. It gives farmers the ability to choose the best conditions for labor efficiency in cultivating a land plot. Local knowledge falls into three categories: maturation process, environment, and biological response. All three involve knowledge of cyclical and seasonal natural phenomena related to the climate and environment of the local flora, which can be considered local phenology. This knowledge supports farmers' resilience during the post-disaster period.

Previous studies on disaster risk reduction and indigenous knowledge have focused on the cultural origins of knowledge and its continuity through generations. The approach of this chapter adds new concepts related to disaster risk reduction science and policies. Biological response knowledge is a more innovative type of knowledge in this field since it is acquired by individuals and is associated with introducing new technology and social institutions. However, a powerful and adaptive aspect of this knowledge creates new capacities to cope with previously unknown conditions.

The three categories of knowledge are integrated into the collective minds of the farmers. Therefore, disaster risk reduction scientists and policymakers should carefully identify the dynamics and complexities of indigenous knowledge and provide robust support for its application in disaster-related circumstances. Agricultural policymakers should encourage the transmission of the maturation process and environmental knowledge as a cultural legacy from one generation to the next, along with the fundamental knowledge of traditional technology. In addition, the dissemination and use of knowledge about biological responses should be encouraged. This knowledge can suggest solutions to farmers facing unforeseen difficulties after a disaster, such as how to resume production even when labor power has been reduced. Some farmers with greater knowledge in this area may hesitate to share it with others because it is directly related to their business. Policymakers involved in disaster risk reduction should help to create opportunities for local people to share knowledge. If these three systemized types of knowledge were spread more widely, they would support a community's adaptation capacity in a post-disaster agricultural setting.

When a tsunami causes severe damage to agriculture, one may regard economic assistance to farmers and civil engineering measurements for farmland as universally applicable physical-economic policies. However, every post-disaster setting requires local solutions. The importance of dynamic and complex indigenous knowledge should be emphasized. It would help convey a wider understanding of the social processes as farmers adapt to post-disaster exigencies with their traditions and innovation. It could also contribute to policy recommendations in different localities.

Notes

1   Sourced from the newspaper *Nihon Keizai Shimbun*, dated 19 April 2011. Accessed 1 January 2022. www.nikkei.com/article/DGXNASDG1902Z_Z10C11A4CC1000/.
2   The fifth report of areas affected by the tsunami by local administrations (18 April 2011) [in Japanese]. Accessed 1 January 2022. www.gsi.go.jp/common/000059939.pdf; population and households affected by the tsunami by local administrations in Miyagi prefecture (2011) [in Japanese]. Accessed 1 January 2022. www.stat.go.jp/info/shinsai/pdf/sinsui04.pdf.

3 Yamamoto chō 2013. Fourth plan of land use by Yamamoto chō [in Japanese]. Accessed 1 January 2022. www.town.yamamoto.miyagi.jp/uploaded/attachment/1073.pdf.

4 Miyagi Ken 2015. Outline of agriculture and rural villages in Miyagi [in Japanese]. Accessed 9 September 2015. www.pref.miyagi.jp/uploaded/attachment/309780.pdf.

5 Accessed 5 August 2022. https://town.yamamoto.miyagi.jp/soshiki/23/2129.html.

6 This related to the post-war Japanese history. The occupation force after WWII in 1940s implemented the agrarian liberation, which allocated the smaller plots to the tenant from the previous landowners. The Japanese government had encouraged this with the agricultural subsidies until the policymakers' recognition in the 2000s of social conditions in aging rural areas and their depopulation (Ohizumi 2014). Farmers themselves had not regarded the fields as a commodity, which prevented the development of larger-scale farming.

6 The norms of recovery among small-scale fisheries

6.1 Collectivism and individualism

The long Pacific coast of Tohoku, in northeast Japan, is well known for the good quality of its fishing grounds, owing to the confluence of warm and cold currents. This area has historically developed the maritime products industry in various ways, which has sustained the recent domestic and international demands of Japanese food. The 3.11 disaster heavily damaged fishery communities and industries. This chapter investigates how the fishery has recovered after the disaster.

Fishing societies are generally individualistic and independent (Acheson 1981). Some reasons include the variability of maritime resources, relative isolation from land, technological responses to uncertain situations, and the common nature of resources (Pollnac 1988). Japanese fishers and their communities are no exception, although it is a rather relative perspective compared to the attributes of peasant societies. (Akimichi 1995; Takakuwa 1994). Individualism is also regarded as a consequence of competitiveness (Jentoft and Davis 1993; Leibbrandt et al. 2013). How do these societies recover from disasters when solidarity is an indispensable requirement for recovery? In what contexts will cooperation occur in a fishing community in the aftermath of a disaster?

One theoretical answer might be the concept of "disaster utopia," which American writer, Rebecca Solnit, describes as a collaborative behavior that temporarily appears among those affected in an emergency but disappears quickly after the emergency has passed. She found an unmet desire for connection, participation, and even altruism in seemingly individualist post-industrial societies and that disaster acts as an opportunity to establish this connection (Solnit 2009, 306).

Some social scientists researching aspects of the 3.11 disaster observed the emergence of numerous simultaneous joint recovery activities in fishery communities soon after the tsunami disaster (Kawashima 2015; Obiya

DOI: 10.4324/9781003348757-6

2016; Sakaguchi 2019; Takano 2013; Ueda and Torigoe 2012; Wilhelm and Delaney 2013; Yoshino 2017). Fishers who acted competitively during "normal" times initiated joint and communal operations once faced with a significant emergency. These findings are significant as a local form of "disaster utopia," but disaster recovery is a long and ongoing process. Researchers have shown that severe conditions remained for more than five years after the disaster (Katayama 2016; Wilhelm 2018). The "disaster-utopia" concept does not explain the prolonged recovery process sufficiently.

Another theoretical explanation for cooperation after a disaster among individualist fishers may be community resilience and social capital. The concept of "resilience," derived initially from ecology, refers to individual or group capacities to deal with, resist, and recover from the effects of disasters (Alexander 2013; Baekes 2008, 73; Oliver-Smith 2009, 14). "Social capital" describes features of social organization, such as networks, norms, and trust, which facilitate action and cooperation for mutual benefit (Putnam 1995, 67). This implies that greater social capital results in greater resilience. Social scientists emphasize the role of social capital in disaster recovery, classified by bonding (emotional connection among individuals), bridging (connection to social groups), and linking (power connection) (Aldrich and Meyer 2014). Some argue that the various types of social organization (or bridging types) take different approaches to leadership for fishery community resilience, while others emphasize the role of outside advocates, linking the success of governmental support in the 3.11 disaster (Kawashima 2015; Obiya 2016; Nagano 2014; Sakaguchi 2019).

The role of social capital or that of the structured social relation is an important aspect of fishery disaster recovery is undeniable; however, fishing technology and resource management should also be considered because a combination of social relations and fish catch affect the recovery process of fishery communities.

The question in this chapter is what sociocultural context could generate the type of solidarity seen in disaster recovery in an everyday fishery setting or an individualist society. If the reason for competitiveness in a fishery society is the conditions related to resources and ecology, how can we explain collaboration in the same socio-ecological context? A previous insightful study on human competitiveness argues that the local work experience resulting from different technologies and socio-ecological factors leads to competitiveness (Leibbrandt et al. 2013, 9307). Given that competitive individualism in fishing societies corresponds to the socio-ecological conditions of resources, cooperative collectivism can occur given certain conditions.

Thus, we do not need to argue for a temporal shift to individual or collective action or a degree of various types of social capital strength; rather, we must explore the conditions under which individualism coexists with collectivism. The relationship between individualism and collectivism can be rephrased as the relationship between competition and cooperation. Most social scientists regard the emergence of cooperation as divergent from competitive behaviors; however, anthropologists have shown that cooperation and competition coexist in all societies (Molina et al. 2017). How can two attributes coexist in fishing societies as a socio-ecological system (Gallopin 1991; Young et al. 2006)?

This chapter uses ethnographical data to explain the process of recovery in small-scale fisheries affected by the 2011 tsunami in Miyagi prefecture and considers the role of local culture as a form of socio-ecological system corresponding to emergency and non-emergency states.

The focus is on small-scale fisheries as examples of fisheries recovery, as approximately 96% of the fishing industry in Tohoku Pacific prefectures (Iwate, Miyagi, Fukushima) is employed in small-scale coastal fisheries (Kase 2012, 26). This is consistent with the global trend: the fishing industry employs approximately 38 million people, with 90% working in small-scale fisheries (Westlund et al. 2007, 13). An examination of the socio-ecological system of small-scale fisheries in Japan, focusing on ethics, technology, socioeconomic relations, and ecology, provides some insights and suggestions for small-scale fisheries' disaster risk reduction in a broader context.

6.2 Pacific Tohoku coast and the 3.11 disaster

The tsunami that struck Japan's Tohoku Pacific coast in 2011 heavily damaged the fishing industry. In the three hardest-hit administrative prefectures (Iwate, Miyagi, and Fukushima prefectures), 18,622 boats and vessels (64%), 260 ports (99%), 35 fishing markets (100%), and 627 processing facilities (84%) were destroyed. The economic loss was calculated to be 11 billion USD (Kase 2012; Wilhelm 2018, 146).[1] In the years after the disaster, the Japanese government implemented various reconstruction policies for public infrastructure and provided financial support for individual fishers.

In the aftermath of the disaster, a new policy was introduced: "special zoning for fishing reconstruction (*suisangyo hukko tokku*)," with a neo-liberal orientation (Nihei 2018; Ryugasaki 2014), or so-called "disaster capitalism" (Klein 2007). In the tsunami-affected areas, policymakers promoted the change in labor organization from family fishing to company-based management or fishery-complex corporations. Under the pretext of the increase in aging fishers and the decline in fishing industry profits, the government intended to weaken fisheries' territorial-use rights. It recommended that external business organizations to participate instead of local fishery associations, which, in the view of policymakers, should result in the decrease of public subsidies (Hamada 2014; Kase 2013). Although many fishers quit their jobs, small-scale fishers with local fishing associations have strongly resisted this neo-liberal policy. These fishers recovered their pre-disaster ways of fishing with some innovations, which was an unexpected result for policymakers (Delaney 2017; Ryugasaki 2014; Ominami et al. 2019; Takano 2013).

Government statistics show a decrease of almost 50% in the number of fishers engaging in aquaculture, although there has been only a 20% decrease in the population of boat fishers. Regardless of the reduction in labor power, in terms of production level, there was an approximately 80% recovery of fishery catches in Iwate and Miyagi prefectures[2] by 2014 (Katayama 2016, 93). What has occurred in fishery communities and industries that cannot be seen in simple catch statistics?

6.3 Fieldwork in the tsunami-affected locus

The field site encompasses two fishing communities located on the coast of southern Miyagi prefecture: Arahama and Isohama. Their coast features a long, flat coastline with a large sandy beach. Due to the flat coastline, there is little local tsunami lore with almost no records of giant tsunamis.[3] Fishery communities are a part of small towns or villages where fishing is one of the local industrial sectors. The main operation is offshore boat fishing and shellfish gathering (Hamada 2014, 213). While some women contribute to the processing and distribution sectors, most men work on larger boats and have limited relationships with community members other than their economic interactions as fishers.

Arahama belongs to Watari Township, and Isohama belongs to Yamamoto Township.[4] The distance between these two communities was almost 15 km, and the 2011 tsunami destroyed nearly all of the houses, boats, and ports in these areas, resulting in many casualties. These communities take part in four main types of fishing: shellfish gathering, fixed-net fishing, cage fishing (a type of lobster pot), and gill net fishing.

The anthropological fieldwork began in Arahama and Isohama in June 2015 and continued until June 2019 with (nearly) monthly visits. The research methods included participant observation and semi-structured interviews with more than 50 individuals, including fishers, local traders, market officers, and local branch representatives of the Miyagi Fisheries Cooperative.[5] Most geographical features of Arahama and Isohama were swept away by the tsunami, and the physical communities disappeared completely. Anglers and other community members then dispersed and moved to villages and towns. Unlike fishers' neighborly relations before the tsunami, their meetings are now limited to fishing operations. Therefore, the field research day-trip visits corresponded to fishing activities rather than home visits. These day-trip visits included participant observation on fishing boats, which usually departed around midnight or at dawn.

Most ethnographic data related to the fishery presented in this chapter are based on fieldwork from Isohama. The scale of business in Isohama is smaller than that in Arahama, making the Isohama region more suitable for exploring the role of culture in post-disaster recovery. Since 2015, repetitive follow-up interviews have been recorded with some fishers and office staff at local fishery cooperatives. In addition, literature covering community history and local government reports on disaster reconstruction in the area were used (Yamamoto 1994, 2018a, 2018b).

6.4 Tsunami scars and emergent correspondence

6.4.1 The local statistics

Isohama is an administrative hamlet within Yamamoto Township; it is located in the southernmost area, bordering Fukushima prefecture. Before the 3.11 disaster, the population comprised 505 people, with 151 households in the year 2010. In 2008, 32 fishing boats were registered and the annual average catch (of both fish and shellfish) was approximately 440 tons (Yamamoto 2018a, 18 and 24).

According to interviews with local fishers, fishing was done on a small scale or at the family level, with no work at the level of larger enterprises. Before the disaster, each household that fished usually owned its own boat; a rough estimate was that about 20% of households were involved in fishing. Most fishers worked in pairs of father and son (or son-in-law). Wives and other family members were not involved in fishing; they were homemakers or worked part-time jobs unrelated to fishing. Before the tsunami, some wives helped their husbands and sons by mending fishing nets in the gardens of their houses. Since the community moved away from the beach after the tsunami, this help no longer takes place. There are no roles or tasks for women in the local fishing processes. The lack of a processing industry meant that fishing did not play an integrated role in the community's economy before and after the disaster. At the time of the disaster, 44 fishers were working in Isohama and 28 boats were registered there. Their catches were seasonal, and they adapted their equipment and practices to the different types of fishing, such as set gill net fishing in spring and autumn, annual gill net fishing, and collecting Sakhalin surf clams in tidal pools. Taken together, these various types of work accounted for most of the fishery production in Isohama and can be considered typical of Japanese commercial fisheries.

The 2011 tsunami destroyed all of the boats in Isohama, except for one moored in a port; nine fishing household members were killed. 20 fishers left the occupation due to the tsunami; however, six newcomers have joined the Isohama fishery since 2011. As of December 2017, 24 fishers worked on 12 boats bought after the tsunami. The youngest boat owner was middle-aged (~42 years old), while the oldest was 72. The age of a fishing crew usually ranges from 18 to 50 years. Given that the total fishery population has decreased significantly since 2011, the arrival of younger newcomers is seen as a positive development.

6.4.2 Joint operations soon after the disaster

Immediately after the disaster, Isohama fishers either moved to governmental temporary evacuation facilities or with relatives. The single miraculously saved boat was brought to Isohama port with the cooperation of local fishers. They were members of the Isohama Fishery Cooperative and shared the fisheries' local territorial-use rights. In May 2011, the government initiated a program to remove the disintegrating concrete block debris along the coastal area using salvaging companies. This was necessary because the tsunami had destroyed the seawalls along the beach and the remains of these structures had been thrown onto the shore. The fishers of Isohama were asked to participate with their boats, a process conducted through the network of local fishery cooperatives. This government reconstruction policy provided fishers with income for their help in the removal of sea debris and the physical reconstruction of fishery infrastructure such as ports and storehouses (Kase 2012; Yamamoto 2018b).

During this process, local fishers had the opportunity to meet other residents, interact, and exchange ideas. According to Mr. Ito (pseudonym), the head of the Isohama Fishermen's Cooperative, the fishers who participated in the garbage collection operation tried to find something they could do as survivors and agreed to fish with fixed nets. They found some ropes and nets in the debris on the beach and repaired these items. Because all the surviving fishers lost their boats, cargo, and nets, they practiced rotating fishing on boats (fixed-net fishing and cage fishing) and unloading on land. Profits were allocated equally among participants. These joint actions continued until 2014–2015. The government provided financial support to fishers to purchase new boats, and in April 2015, local fishers began to purchase their boats. The owners of the new boats then left the joint fishing operations and pursued individual fishing. The Isohama case illustrates that cooperative fishing (collectivism) with egalitarian profit distribution occurred soon after the initial emergency. Egalitarian outcomes connect solidarity (Greenwood 1988). These joint operations enhanced a sense of fellowship among the local fishers and resulted in each restart of fishing after the interval due to the disaster. This outcome is similar to previous studies on Sanriku community-based fisheries (Ueda and Torigoe 2012; Yoshino 2017). However, while those communities faced a "temporal disaster utopia," the next section describes Isohama's continuing recovery process in ethnographic detail.

6.5 Individual and group fisheries in a non-emergency

6.5.1 The contrasting calendar and profit distribution

There are two groups of Isohama fishers. One group consists of individual fishers, based on family pairs, and a second group consists of cooperative fishing undertaken by several families.[6] If the joint operation symbolized temporal solidarity explained by the concept of the disaster utopia, does individual fishing on each boat indicate evidence of completion of recovery?

Individual fishing households conduct gill net fishing in offshore areas (Figure 6.1). The primary targets are flounder or Japanese rockfish and whitebait during the season. They usually leave the port around midnight and return to the harbour in the morning. The unit of operation is the family, and it is this family household that undertakes the risks and collects profits.

Group fishing mainly engages in fixed-net fishing and shellfish gathering. This joint operation follows a precise seasonal calendar: spring fixed-net fishing occurs from April to July for Japanese sea bass, repair of the netting takes place in August and September, autumn fixed-net fishing takes place from October to December for salmon, and the gathering of Sakhalin surf clam takes place from December to March. Two teams, each consisting of three families, work in a joint operation, and all participants share in the profits equally.[7] At the same time, these fishers engage in individual fishing in their spare time after the completion of the joint operations. This may include cage fishing for crabs from April to June and fishing for octopus from October to November. Fishers sometimes take part in gill net fishing in July (Figure 6.2).

The practices of the individualist and collectivist fishers contrast in terms of un-demarcated or demarcated fishing calendars and competitive (une-qual) or income-equal profit distributions. The two types of local practices were not invented after the disaster, they existed before. According to the fishers, the joint operation during the emergency was not a "disaster utopia" but rather an extended manner of group fishing.

Joint operations are also undertaken during the annual festival, when fishers pray collectively for a good catch at the local Shinto shrine in January and at the general meeting of the Isohama Shipowners' Association

Figure 6.1 Fisherman operating alone at the gill net fishing (19 July 2018)
Source: Hiroki Takakura

Figure 6.2 Fix-net fishing in autumn (7 November 2018)
Source: Hiroki Takakura

in March. The leader of the local fisher cooperative organizes these events and representatives from every family participate in them. Aside from these events, most fishers rarely converse with others, apart from their fellow boat members. Fishers work separately, except in emergencies. This is partially because the individual fishers and the group fishers usually have different operation times. Another reason is the closure of the market auction at the Isohama Port.[8] Each fisher and group needs to find a broker to make a sale, consequently reducing the opportunities for communication among them after unloading. The market cessation was a critical event, as many felt that the recovery from the disaster had not been completed.

6.5.2 Why has the collectivist fishery not disappeared?

If the fishery societies were inherently individualistic, independent, and egalitarian, why has the opposite character been sustained in the group fishery? This question is addressed with field data. The first case is a complaint from a young fisher who was employed as a member of the group fishery after the disaster. His attitude seems to display the typical characteristics of an individualist fisher:

> Fixed-net fishing and cage fishing are easier than gill net fishing because we do not need to embark at midnight. If my father and I worked together, because of our different physical capabilities, I could hardly see how the business could be expanded. What we can do depends on the range of cooperation. [I have] no perspective on big money and success. No greed. If I moved to gill net fishing, I would need knowledge of many types of nets depending on the fish type.
>
> (Interview, 8 June 2018)

The young fisher recognized fixed-net fishing, a tool promoting collectivism, as a relatively easier way to participate as a newcomer. However, the economic return from this type of work would be limited due to families' egalitarian sharing of profits. He regards gill net fishing, a tool that promotes individualism, as requiring more skills. From this perspective, group fishing could be an elementary stage, while individual fishing represents an advanced stage or development from a collective/cooperative to individual/competitive fishing.

   However, older and more experienced fishers have different opinions on economic stability and labor efficiency:

> Fixed-net fishing requires time and effort. However, once well set, the working time at sea for a round of this fishing would be two hours.

Gill net fishing requires at least four hours or more for a round. One needs to perform net management after every haul. In addition, in terms of economic expense, one must often buy a new gill net, and gill net fishing requires more gasoline. Fixed-net fishing is economical. If we complete a round, one may engage in other tasks, such as individual cage fishing. Certainly, the gill net fishers are able to keep their own profits, but the catch changes every day they go out. It is like gambling. However, the catch in fixed-net fishing is stable enough to sustain a household economy, and we can predict how much we will make.

(Interview, 22 June 2018)

In addition, the elder fisher refuted the younger's opinion that deeper knowledge is necessary for fixed-net fishing rather than gill net fishing because the former has a complex structure.

There is a different reason for the survival of the collectivist way: the price of a fixed shore net is very high, approximately 20,000,000 JPY (approximately 190,000 USD). Therefore, several families purchased this equipment before the disaster. The current relationship between these families, who engage with fixed-net fishing, could span several generations. Mr. Iida (pseudonym), a fisherman in his 60s, who is vice chair of the local fishery cooperative, told me that joint fishing began during his father's generation. He hopes that joint fixed-net fishing will continue into the next generation as his son-in-law and other sons work together. They believe that close associations that share the risk should continue long term. The advantage of the group fishery is that the compensation it provides is not only steady income but also a long-term trusting relationship.

6.5.3 Sea and sentiment

While economic stability and long-term social capital might be reasonable explanations for the group fishery, what are the other drivers of collectivism? First, it is important to discuss the issue of the fishing grounds. The Isohama Fishery Cooperative's fishing grounds are legally acknowledged as a territorial use of fishing rights, and all members of the Isohama branch of the fishing cooperative have equal usage rights. Interestingly, the two groups use different areas of the surrounding ocean according to their fishing methods.

Figure 6.3 illustrates the fishing ground map of the Isohama fishers from March to November 2018. The GPS data were collected during my participant observations on boats conducting shellfish gathering, fixed-net fishing, cage fishing, and gill net fishing.[9] The fishers conceptualized space in the ocean according to the distance from the beach: *nada* as shore areas

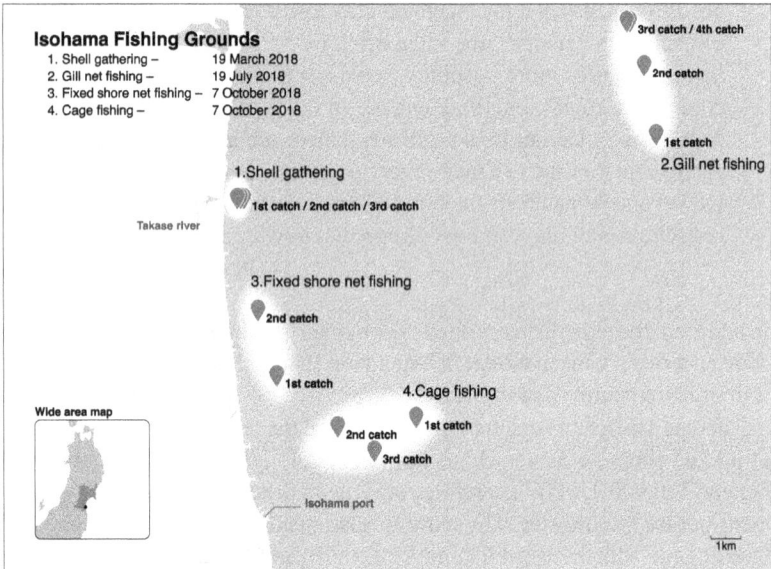

Figure 6.3 Fishing ground map of Isohama fishers from March to November 2018
Source: Hiroki Takakura

for shellfish gathering and fixed-net fishing, and *oki* as offshore for gill net fishing. In general, the joint operations of shellfish gathering and fixed-net fishing are undertaken closer to the beach, and individual gill net fishing operates further offshore. Cage fishing occurs between these two areas.

A fisher, aged 50 years old, who returned to Isohama from the city after the disaster and chose fishing as an occupation, told me of the advantage of fishing on the safer shore areas. Needless to say, shore fishing is generally quiet and safe, while offshore fishing is relatively rough and dangerous. Does the group fisher who works in a relatively safe condition with outcome equality pursue economic stability? Fieldwork shows that collectivists have several drivers beyond safety and money. There is, for example, the case of another fisher, Hiroshi Hamamoto (pseudonym), who is 37 years old. He was born in Yoshida Hamlet, which is 10 km north of Isohama and in the next township, and has no local fishery:

> When I was depressed after the disaster, . . . my father-in-law asked me to become a fisher . . . I do not consider fishing to be tough work. Making money is difficult to achieve. Fishing offers a good income. I am

satisfied with it. In addition, salmon in fixed-net fishing is marvellous. In my first experience, I was very impressed by salmon fishing.

(Interview, 8 June 2018)

Feelings of success expressed by new fishers include satisfaction with income and a deep emotional connection with salmon fishing. The importance of this emotion in cooperative fishing using fixed-net fishing is not to be underestimated. All fishers, whether newcomer or veteran, expect the success of the massive catch through joint action.

The local historiography dates the pre-modern harbour and the related facilities of this region (both of Isohama and Arahama) to the mid-17th century and the statistics of the salmon catch at least to 1907 (Inoue 2014; Watari 1977; Yamamoto 1994; see also Takahashi 2015). One well-informed fisher, Watase Suizo (pseudonym, born in 1953), described that the fixed-net fishing for salmon started here in 1895, before which the locals used the coastal dragnet (23 July 2015). With such a long history of salmon fishing, the regional cuisine has developed a unique local dish of *harakomeshi*, or boiled rice mixed with female salmon after removing the roe.[10] This local culinary innovation represents prefectural cuisine, but its origin is in Isohama and Arahama. The local elementary school has a special visiting program with the Isohama Fishery Cooperative during the salmon fishing season. Some fishers teach children about their history and food culture.

Collective fishing satisfies economic profit and the emotional sentiments inherent in catch prosperity and the sense of involvement in local history and economics. Risk avoidance and self-fulfillment are key to the continuation of group fisheries in non-emergency situations. Individualists and collectivists base their fishing practices on different rationales.

6.6 The fishing continuum in the local environment

What lessons can we learn from these types of fishing? As described previously, Isohama fishers conduct four types of fishing: shellfish gathering, fixed-net fishing, cage fishing, and gill net fishing. Table 6.1 presents the typology of fishing in this community. Based on the field interviews and participant observations, these four types of fishing have been classified based on factors such as preparation and maintenance of gear, operation time at sea, gear investment costs, income, economic incentive, style of management, and the degree of participation for newcomers. The different orientations can clearly be understood. Gill net and cage fishing are competitive, individualistic, hard to enter, short term, and provide unequal income. Fixed-net fishing and shellfish gathering are cooperative, collective, and relatively easy to enter, have a long-term perspective, and have

Table 6.1 Typology of local fishing methods in Isohama

	Gill net	*Cage*	*Fixed-net*	*Shell gathering*
Preparation by every operation	Complicated	Less complicated	Simple	Simple
Maintenance of gear by operation	Difficult	Less difficult	Easy	Easy
Operation time in sea	Long	Long	Short	Short
Gear Investment	Inexpensive	Inexpensive	Expensive	Expensive
Income	Unstable	Unstable	Stable	Stable
Economic incentive	Competitive	Competitive	Outcome equality	Outcome equality
Management	Family	Family	Group	Community
Participation for new comers	Difficult	Less difficult	Less difficult	Less difficult
Fishing grounds	Offshore (Oki)	Near offshore (Oki)	Near coast (Nada)	Nearer coast (Nada)

income equality. Interestingly, this orientation corresponds to differences in fishing grounds. Generally, competitive, individualistic fishing operates offshore, whereas cooperative, collective fishing occurs near the coast. The local terms used for the two types of fishing also signify the distance from the beach.

The two fishing orientations do not compete with each other but are harmoniously separated by socio-ecological conditions. The closer the fishing ground, the more stable the catches and the less skilled work is required, even for newcomers. This is due to cooperation in work and equal distribution of income. The more distant the fishing grounds, the higher the risk, catch yields, and skilled labor required, which is based on individual discretion for both labor and profit. The research questions in this chapter are how the two contradictory attributes of competitive-individualist and cooperative-collectivist are embedded in society and how this combination works in prolonged disaster recovery. This chapter shows that although the two different types of ethics and behavior of competitive/individualist and cooperative/collective are seemingly in conflict, they are interdependent, as reflected by the local fishing culture and ecology. A fishing continuum has formed, connecting competitive individualism to cooperative collectivism. During normal times, the four local fishing methods take place in different locations according to socio-ecological conditions in the continuum.

The success of the "disaster utopia" in this artisanal fishery lies in the local culture. The effects of government policies or other external factors as preconditions for resilience should also be revisited. For instance, the local participation policy in sea debris removal soon after the tsunami disaster provided an opportunity for fishers to meet and discuss viable options for the future. This was particularly important considering the scattered living conditions after evacuation. Another important policy was financial support for fishing boats and infrastructure. The enhancement of local communication among victims and their physical environment improved as people found their path to recovery in conformity with the local culture. The policies supporting the existing fishery organization, rather than the neo-liberal one, were effective for disaster recovery in the Isohama case.

As in previous studies, the joint temporal operation in Isohama during the emergency phase is confirmed as a disaster utopia. The local fishery cooperative functioned with social capital for resilience, providing enhanced social ties among fishers. They harnessed related government policies to increase their social capital; however, those two aspects do not sufficiently explain why individualists collaborated in the prolonged process. Rather, the local context is the reason that some individualist fishers require the safe labor conditions, the economic stability, the self-esteem involved in local history and economics, and the emotional sentiment in the cooperative-collective fishery.

When an emergency occurred, solidarity became necessary among the fishers; they switched to a cooperative and outcome-equal fishing mode. When there were signs of recovery, some fishers moved to an individualistic and competitive mode, but others continued to engage in more collective work. There is logic to the two modes of behavior among artisanal fishers. It would be difficult to ensure resilience over a prolonged recovery process if there was only one mode (individualistic and competitive) in their fishing tradition.

It is important to emphasize the significance of the two modes of behavior that spontaneously coexist, even in normal times. This is embedded in social and technological conditions as well as in environmental conditions. It must be noted that the catch targets of fixed-net fishing are salmon and Japanese sea bass, which are seasonal migratory fish. The amounts of these fish are sizable, and the fishing strategy aims at a stable catch by using larger and more complex gear and cooperation. In this way, fishers manage diverse maritime resources using different strategies. While local fishers engage in cooperative/collectivist fishing for migratory catches, they participate in competitive/individualist fishing for sedentary fish. The typical migratory fishes are salmon in autumn and sea bass in spring, whereas sedentary catches include flounder, octopus, crab, and rockfish. The exception to this dichotomy is the harvesting of Sakhalin surf clams, for which the joint operation of a pool production system that replaced individual fishing in 1978, due to overharvesting (Sasaki 1993, 67). The fishing community institutionalizes the competitive distribution for sedentary fish with less resource fluctuation (stable), while outcome-equal distribution has been adopted for migratory fish with larger resource fluctuations (unstable). This represents a strategy to enhance competitiveness in a stable resource condition while reducing the individual risk with an affluent but unstable resource condition.

A comparison can be made to the anthropology of sedentary and storage hunter-gatherers in the northern Pacific coastal peoples, demonstrating the importance of seasonal affluent migratory resources for sedentary adaptation with social stratification even within hunter-gatherer societies without food production. Family-based occupational differentiation can also be observed in these societies (Flannery and Marcus 2012, 62–86; Testart 1995, 185; Watanabe 1986). Egalitarian hunter-gatherers could change to become non-egalitarian according to ecology and resource conditions, particularly due to changes in food resource affluence and the cold climate necessary for food preservation. The anthropology of northern Pacific coast fishers shows that seasonal prosperity affects the socio-ecological balance and leads to a shift from an egalitarian to a socially stratified society. In the current case study of artisan fisheries in Tohoku, Japan, seasonal affluence allows cooperative collectivism as an alternative norm and behavior in contrast to the competitive individualism of the generalized fishing society. We may observe these different methods in contrast between group and individual fishing. If the disturbance of the socio-ecological equilibrium were emphasized as a regular or expected event, the fishers would coexist with these two different ways of individual and group fishing, or cooperative and competitive norms. The coexistence of conflicting norms and behaviors in a community helps people fish and diversify their economies during times when there is no emergency. Simultaneously, it also forms emergency-related cooperation and autonomous recovery to the normal mode without any government interventionist policy.

6.7   Conclusions

This chapter aims to explain the local mechanism of the prolonged recovery process of artisanal fisheries in Tohoku, Japan. Here, the process contrasts with that of a disaster utopia, which some researchers have seen following catastrophic events. While collaborative behaviors among the fishers in this study can be seen as a type of disaster utopia or a temporary solidarity collaboration, they should be also be understood as a part of the local resilience process, which functions not only by social capital but also by the local socio-ecological system. Understanding how resilience can exist in a prolonged recovery process can contribute to the research on disaster risk management and reveal how the advantages and vulnerabilities of resilient mechanisms can lead to effective policies.

This chapter emphasized that the key to resilience in the studied areas is the local tradition of fishing using two different modes of behavior and ethics. This dichotomy has been formed by both the environmental context of two different maritime resources (sedentary and migratory) and the technological aspects of fishing. The ethnic balance between individualism and collectivism is decisively coordinated in an area's socio-ecological system. In this regard, the conclusions of previous research on human competitiveness being determined by local experiences of different technologies and socio-ecological factors are supported (Leibbrandt et al. 2013).

However, in terms of disaster risk management, this chapter contests a monolithic perspective, emphasizing either competitive or collective activity. Harvest of marine resources can be regulated by socio-ecological systems that determine whether the harvest is suitable for a competitive or cooperative fishery. This determination corresponds to the spatial use of the sea. Fishers can choose the type of work they prefer according to their circumstances. Competitive individualism is associated with higher risk and income, while cooperative collectivism is associated with stability, moderate income, self-esteem, and feelings more appropriate for newcomers or older fishers. Ecology and social demand for marine resources dictate which method – individualism or collectivism – people will choose. Rather than the monolithic conceptualization of the social attributes of a fishing society, the perspective of family-based occupational differentiation and the changing preferences of fishers according to various conditions are required to study disaster risk reduction. Social scientists and policymakers engaged in disaster research should avoid these monolithic perspectives and carefully understand the affected community through pluralistic and flexible perspectives. While policymakers may prefer a simplistic, essentialist view of society for the quick and effective implementation of disaster risk management, I recommend considering the pluralistic conceptualization of social characteristics in the target community. This can contribute to the development of disaster management policies for small-scale fisheries.

Furthermore, the availability of multiple resources allows fishers to choose their resources. They can choose which practices to engage in during normal times, whereas solidarity and cooperative collectivism are required in response to a disaster. The multiple-resource strategy based on maritime biodiversity in a small-scale fishery is crucial for resilience in the face of uncertainty about disastrous events, which generates solidarity. Disaster risk management for small-scale fisheries should encourage their capabilities to engage in diverse fishing methods, such as individualism and collectivism, for the multiple marine resources in their community. This capability is crucial for disaster recovery. The loss of diversity, changes in the consumer market, and the environment may all affect the vulnerability of small-scale fisheries. Policymakers should thus carefully observe these aspects and intervene on time against adverse repercussions. These recommendations are based on the premise that governmental financial support for the means of production, such as boats, and the maritime biological diversity corresponds to the local fishing tradition.

Notes

1 The Japanese government reported damage to fisheries during the 2011 disaster. Accessed 1 January 2022. http://dl.ndl.go.jp/view/download/digidepo_6008618_po_03_p17-22.pdf?contentNo=4&alternativeNo=>p.19.
2 Fukushima prefecture has a completely different pattern than the other two areas because of the ongoing nuclear radiation.
3 Tsunami engineers and geologists started to explore the preceding giant tsunami, the Jogan tsunami of AD 869, before 2011 (Sugawara 2013).
4 Yamamoto Township became an independent municipality from Watari Township in 1955.
5 Japan Fisheries (JF) is Japan's National Fisheries Cooperative Association. JF Miyagi represents the prefectural-wide Fisheries Cooperative Association founded in 2007 by a merger of all cooperatives in the prefecture.
6 Four families engage in individual fishing, and six families engage in group fishing.
7 The fishers have a strict rule for the minimum landing size for catches of Sakhalin surf clams and have adopted a pool account, allowing all the members of the group fishing pool to share the total profit. Pool accounting began in the 1970s due to resource conservation (Abe et al. 2007; Sasaki 1993).
8 The catch of Isohama fishers is sold in the city in Fukushima prefecture, due to its close proximity, rather than to Miyagi prefecture, as was the practice before the disaster. The brokers from Fukushima participated in the market auction in Isohama. Due to the nuclear accident, a decrease in the number of brokers and fish demand in Fukushima did not allow fishers to make ends meet at the Isohama market auction.
9 Unfortunately, I failed to collect GPS data on spring fixed-net fishing (22 June 2018) because of technical issues.
10 Salmon roe, or *sujiko*, is a different commodity that can be sold separately.

7 Conclusions

This book explored the role of culture in disaster risk reduction and the way anthropologists who face a disaster at home engage with it. Two typical approaches to disaster risk reduction are the universal or cultural models. Instead, I have the approach "with the people in" focusing on the recovery process of the affected communities after the 3.11 disaster. Beyond the local knowledge and behaviors directly connected to disaster preparedness, the local capacities that emerged in the recovery process were uncovered.

My work was also concerned with how to communicate these findings to policymakers. Disaster anthropology should be intended as an applied science. Scientists are expected to engage in disaster recovery and the mitigation of harmful effects of the disaster. In this context, anthropologists can offer a relevant contribution, especially considering those who suffered disasters at home. Here, I draw lessons from each chapter and summarize recommendations to both policymakers and anthropologists.

Chapter 2 described a disaster documentation project in the Tohoku University community. An anthropologist who faces a disaster at home can start a documentation project to report the diverse experiences of the victims, starting with colleagues or their loved ones. The project has a performative function in sharing and elaborating others' experiences and encouraging solidarity. Anthropologists and disaster policymakers emphasize the importance of self-documentation projects involving various groups.

Chapter 3 concerned the experience of conduct and execution of a commissioned project on intangible cultural heritage in collaboration with the local administration. Most anthropologists confirm their capabilities to examine all matters regarding people and cultures from any angle. However, I believe that only an expert in the cultural aspects of a particular region can offer such a relevant contribution once a disaster happens in that region for the analysis to be more effective. Practical and immediate contributions to recovery are required at disaster sites. Participant observations

DOI: 10.4324/9781003348757-7

and unstructured interviews from an unfamiliar scholar irritated the survivors and disturbed their well-being in the shelters. If this is not the case, it is preferable to establish a collaboration with the local administration. One possible task for anthropologists is to preserve cultural heritage during disasters. The government expects anthropologists to have expertise in intangible cultural heritage; thus, we should not hesitate to collaborate with the administration or government to achieve these aims.

Chapter 4 examined two folk performing arts in the afflicted communities to explore their role in recovery. Intangible cultural heritage provides a sense of routine to survivors, which is easily lost in unfamiliar circumstances or in the shelter. The folk performing arts also give these communities a sense of the structural time that enforces the diverse forms of social exchange and values to adapt to new conditions. Intangible cultural heritage is important not because of the heritage itself but because of its catalytic function that enforces community resilience. This is why policymakers should include the cultural heritage survey as a standard tool in the reconstruction process, in collaboration with anthropologists.

Chapter 5 analyzed local agricultural knowledge and its function during the recovery. This knowledge is both traditional and informed by the contemporary technological features of science. Some knowledge is collectively transmitted as a local tradition; in contrast, individuals innovatively invent other information. Rather than extrapolating specific knowledge to avoid natural hazards, I discovered how local farmers mobilized their knowledge under post-disaster conditions. While it might be difficult to share knowledge within the community because some information is closely linked to business success, policymakers can create opportunities to encourage the value of local knowledge for the affected farmers.

Chapter 6 examined the background of local solidarity among individual fishers. The Japanese government boosted the policy of disaster capitalism, modifying the "low-productivity," small-scale fishery management, and reorganizing it in large profit-making cooperatives. The policy faced strong opposition from the surviving fishers and their associations. The focus of the chapter was on how fishers balanced between collective and individual activities in the context of fishery technology and the local maritime ecology. Multiple resource strategies, based on maritime biodiversity, could generate solidarity. The recommendation to policymakers is to encourage the potentiality of the local socio-ecological system to boost their ways of recovery. Disaster capitalism hampers producers' survival.

The government tends to give priority to disaster recovery policies concerning primary tasks, such as infrastructure, medical care, and employment, thus giving limited attention to culture. Some may think that only rich governments can afford cultural preservation in the face of disaster losses. This book critically rejects that idea.

All governments and disaster agencies should take measures for disaster recovery using the local culture to alleviate people's suffering. The self-documentation project and intangible cultural heritage survey could be some options that are easy to introduce. While I do not deny the importance of measures for cultural heritage against disasters, I insist that affected people have the capacity to recover in their own way, to which policymakers should pay attention. Culture provides a framework for self-reflection to adapt to post-disaster settings.

Anthropologists can undertake the role of exploring the local ways of resilience in different conditions. I do not claim that culture is an absolute prescription; however, there is a context in which it works well if people want to use it. Anthropologists should slowly and carefully discern and collaborate with people, practitioners, organizations, and governments. The humbleness against the "gold rush" of post-disaster research is a clue to success for disaster anthropology projects because it is not only an ethical norm but also a key for reliance with people and practitioners.

References

Abe, T., O. Akira, and K. Inoue. 2007. Resource conservation type of fishery for Sakhalin surf clam. *Fukushima daigaku chiiki sozo* 19 (1): 91–95. Fukishima: Fukushima University. [In Japanese]

Abu-Lughod, L. 1996. Writing against culture. In *Recapturing anthropology: Working in the present*. R. G. Fox, ed., 137–162. Santa Fe: School of American Research Press.

Acheson, J. M. 1981. The anthropology of fishing. *Annual Review of Anthropology* 10: 275–316.

Akimichi, T. 1995. *Kaiyo minzokugaku* [Maritime anthropology]. Tokyo: Tokyo University Press. [In Japanese]

Aldrich, D., and M. Meyer. 2014. Social capital and community resilience. *American Behavioral Scientist* 59 (2): 254–269. DOI: 10.1177/0002764214550299

Alexander, D. 2012. Our starting point. *International Journal of Disaster Risk Reduction* 1: 1–4.

Alexander, D. 2013. Resilience and disaster risk reduction: An etymological journey. *Natural Hazards and Earth System Sciences* 13 (11). DOI: 10.5194/nhess-13-2707-2013

Appadurai, A. 1988. Putting hierarchy in its place. *Cultural Anthropology* 3: 36–49. DOI: 10.1525/can.1988.3.1.02a00040

Asahishinbun. 1995. *Jinruigaku ga wakaru* [Understanding anthropology]. Tokyo: Asashi Shinbun. [In Japanese]

Baekes, F. 2008. *Scared ecology* (2nd edition). New York and London: Routledge.

Bankoff, G., T. Cannon, F. Kruger, and E. Schipper. 2015. Introduction: Exploring the links between cultures and disasters. In *Cultures and disasters: Understanding cultural framings in disaster risk reduction*. G. B. F. Kruger, T. Cannon, B. Orlowski, and E. Schipper, eds., 1–16. London and New York: Routledge.

Barnard, A. 2000. *Social anthropology: A concise introduction for students*. Taunton: Studymate.

Beck, U. 1998. *Risikogesellschaft auf dem Weg in eine andere Moderne*. Azuma Ren and Ito Midori, trans. Tokyo: Hosei Daigaku Syuppankai. [In Japanese]

Befu, H. 1971. *Japan: An anthropological introduction*. San Francisco: Chandler Publishing Co.

Boret, S. P., and A. Shibayama. 2016. Archiving and memorializing disasters: Report of a UN international workshop. *Journal of Disaster Research* 11 (3): 437–442.10.20965/jdr.2016.p0437

Boret, S. P., and A. Shibayama. 2018. The roles of monuments for the dead during the aftermath of the Great East Japan Earthquake. *International Journal of Disaster Risk Reduction* 29: 55–62.

Cadwell, P. 2019. Foreign residents' experiences of the flyjin phenomenon during the 2011 Great East Japan Earthquake. In *Crisis and disaster in Japan and New Zealand*. S. Bouterey and L. Marceau, eds., 59–78. Singapore: Palgrave Macmillan. DOI: 10.1007/978-981-13-0244-2_5.

Clifford, J. 1986. Introduction: Partial truths. In *Writing culture: The poetics and politics of ethnography*. James Clifford and George E. Marcus, eds., 1–26. Berkeley: University of California Press.

Delaney, A. E. 2017. Waves of change: Adaptation and innovation among Japanese fisheries cooperative members in the post-3.11era. *Northeast Asian Studies* 21: 111–129. hdl.handle.net/10097/00105271

Douglas, M., and A. Wildavsky. 1983. *Risk and culture: An essay on the selection of technical and environmental dangers*. Berkeley: University of California Press.

Embree, J. 2010 (1946). *A Japanese village: Suye Mura*. New York: Routledge.

Evans-Pritchard, E. E. 1969 (1940). *The Nuer: A description of the modes of livelihood and political institutions of a Nilotic People*. New York and Oxford: Oxford University Press.

Fabian, J. 1983. *Time and the other: How anthropology makes its object*. New York: Columbia University Press.

Falk, M. L. 2010. Recovery and Buddhist practices in the aftermath of the tsunami in Southern Thailand. *Religion* 40 (2): 96–103.

Field, L. W., and R. G. Fox. 2009. Introduction: How does anthropology work today? In *Anthropology put to work*. L. W. Field and R. G. Fox, eds., 1–19. New York: Berg.

Flannery, K., and J. Marcus. 2012. *The creation of inequality: How our prehistoric ancestors set the stage for monarchy, slavery, and empire*. Cambridge, MA: Harvard University Press.

Fukishima ken. 1964. *Fukushimaken shi 23 kan, Minzoku* [The history of Fukushima prefecture, 23 volume, Folk culture]. Fukushima: Fukushima Ken. [In Japanese]

Gaillard, J. C., M. Fordham, and K. Sanz. 2015. Culture, gender and disaster: From vulnerability to capacities. In *Cultures and disasters: Understanding cultural framings in disaster risk reduction*. G. B. F. Kruger, T. Cannon, B. Orlowski, and E. Schipper, eds., 222–234. London and New York: Routledge.

Gaillard, J. C., and C. Gomez. 2015. Post-disaster research: Is there gold worth the rush? *Jàmbá: Journal of Disaster Risk Studies* 7 (1): 1–6.

Gallopin, G. C. 1991. Human dimensions of global change: Linking the global and the local processes. *International Social Science Journal* 130: 707–718.

Gerster, J. 2019. Hierarchies of affectedness: Kizuna, perceptions of loss, and social dynamics in post-3.11 Japan. *International Journal of Disaster Risk Reduction* 41. DOI: 10.1016/j.ijdrr.2019.101304

Gill, T. 2013. This spoiled soil: Place, people and community in an irradiated village in Fukushima Prefecture. In *Japan copes with calamity*. Tom Gill, Brigitte Steger, and David Slater, eds., 201–234. Oxford: Peter Lang.

Gill, T., B. Steger, and D. Slater, eds. 2013a. *Higashi nihon daishinsai no jinruigaku* [Anthropology of great East Japan]. Kyoto: Jinbunsyoin. [In Japanese]

Gill, T., B. Steger, and D. Slater, eds. 2013b. *Japan copes with calamity: Ethnographies of the earthquake, tsunami, and nuclear disasters of March 2011*. Oxford: Peter Lang.

Gill, T., B. Steger, and D. Slater. 2015. The 3.11 disasters. In *Japan, copes with calamity*. T. Gill, B. Steger, and D. Slater, eds., 3–24. Oxford: Peter Lang.

Greenwood, D. 1988. Egalitarianism or solidarity in Basque industrial cooperatives: The FAGOR Group of Mondragon. In *Rules, decisions, and inequality in egalitarian societies*. J. Flanagan and S. Rayner, eds., 43–69. Aldershot: Avebury.

Gruber, J. W. 1970. Ethnographic salvage and the shaping of anthropology. *American Anthropologist* 72 (6): 1289–1299. DOI: 10.1525/aa.1970.72.6.02a00040.

Hamada, T. 2014. *Gyogyo to shinsai* [Fishery and disasters]. Tokyo: Misuzu Syobo. [In Japanese]

Hashimoto, H. 2015. *Shinsai to geinō: Chiiki saisei no gendōryoku* [Disaster and local performing arts]. Tokyo: Maruzen. [In Japanese]

Hashimoto, H., and I. Hayashi, eds. 2016. *Saigai bunka no keisyo to sozo* [Tradition and innovation of disaster culture]. Kyoto: Rinkawa shoten. [In Japanese]

Hayakawa, K. 1973 (1958). Inasaku no shūzoku: Tane erabi kara kariage made [Custom of rice cultivation: From the seed rice selection to harvest]. In *Hayakawa Kōtarō Zenshū 7 kan.*, 497–543. Tokyo: Miraisha. [In Japanese]

Hayashi, I., ed. 2010. *Shizen saigai to fukkō shien* [Natural disaster and recovery support] Tokyo: Akashishoten. [In Japanese]

Hayashi, I. 2012. Folk performing art in the aftermath of the Great East Japan Earthquake. *Asian Anthropology* 11 (1): 75–87.

Hayashi, I., S. Kimura, Y. Suzuki, and H. Takakura. 2016. Kadai kenkyu kondaikai houkoku, Saigai no jinruigaku [Activity report of disaster anthropology in Japanese Society of Cultural Anthropology]. *Japanese Journal of Cultural Anthropology* 81–2: 338–343. [In Japanese]

Hendry, J. 2016. *Sharing our worlds* (3rd edition). New York: New York University Press.

Hidaka, S., ed. 2012. *Kioku wo tsunagu. Tsunami saigai to bunka isan* [Memories contexualized: Tsunami disaster and cultural heritage]. Senri-Osaka: Senri Bunka Zaidan. [In Japanese]

Higuchi, Y. 2011. The restoration from the great East Japan earthquake: Employment support and utilization of statistics. *Trends in the Sciences* 16 (12): 92–95. [In Japanese] DOI: 10.5363/tits.16.12_92.

Hiwasaki, L., E. Luna, Symasidik, and R. Shaw. 2014. Process for integrating local and indigenous knowledge with science for hydro-meteorological disaster risk reduction and Climate Change adaptation in coastal and small island communities. *International Journal of Disaster Risk Reduction* 10: 15–27. DOI: 10.1016/j.ijdrr.2014.07.007

Hodgson, S. M., and Z. Irving. 2007. Policy and its exploration. In *Policy reconsidered: Meanings, politics and practices*. S. M. Hodgson and Z. Irving, eds., 1–17. Bristol: Policy Press.

Hoffman, S. M., and A. Oliver-Smith, eds. 2002. *Catastrophe and culture: The anthropology of disaster*. Santa Fe: School of American Research Press.

Horikawa, N. 2016. Displacement and hope after adversity: Narratives of evacuees following the Fukushima nuclear accident. In *Unravelling the Fukushima disaster*. M. Yamakawa and D. Yamamoto, eds., 66–78. New York: Routledge.

Huntington, S. P. 2000. Cultures count. In *Culture matters: How values shape human progress*. L. E. Harrison and S. P. Huntington, eds., xiii–xvi. New York: Basic Books.

Ichinosawa, J. 2010. From danger to risk: Japanese residents and reputational disaster in Phuket after the 2004 Indian Ocean tsunami. *Bulletin of the National Museum of Ethnology* 34 (3): 521–574. [In Japanese]

Iizuka, A. 2021. Local performing arts and recovery from the Great East Japan Earthquake and Tsunami. *International Journal of Disaster Risk Reduction* 63. DOI: 10.1016/j.ijdrr.2021.102446.

Ikeda, Y. 2013. The construction of risk and the resilience of Fukushima in the aftermath of the nuclear power plant accident. In *Japan copes with calamity*. T. Gill, B. Steger, and D. Slater, eds., 151–176. Oxford: Peter Lang Publishing.

Imahashi, E. 2008. *Foto riterasii: hodo syasin to yomu rinri* [Photo Literacy: Journalism Photography and Ethics]. Tokyo: Chuokoronsha. [In Japanese]

Ingold, T. 2018. *Anthropology: Why it matters*. Cambridge: Polity Press.

Inoue, T. 2014. *Arahama minato no nigiwai* [History of Arahama]. Sendai: Banzanbou. [In Japanese]

Irikura, K. 2012. What should we do for reducing mega-disaster risk and building disaster-resilient societies? *Trends in the Sciences* 17 (8): 14–19. [In Japanese] DOI: 10.5363/tits.17.8_14.

Ishikawa, M. 2011. Focusing on the process of making the restoration plan in the damaged area. *Trends in Sciences* 16 (12): 8–14. [In Japanese] DOI: 10.5363/tits.16.12_8.

Ishimoto, T. 2014. Succession of rice farming on terraced fields. *Bulletin of the Japanese Society of Folklore* 279: 1–32. [In Japanese]

Itani, J. 1982. *Daikanbatsu: Turukana nikki* [Great drought: A description of the Turkana]. Tokyo: Shinchosha. [In Japanese]

Iwagaki, T., T. Tsujiuchi, and A. Ogihara. 2017. Social capital and mental health in a major disaster: Findings and suggestions from the survey and social-support after Fukushima nuclear disaster. *Japanese Journal of Psychosomatic Medicine* 57 (10): 1013–1019. [In Japanese]

Jenkins, R. 2007. The meaning of policy/policy as meaning. In *Policy reconsidered: Meanings, politics and practices*. S. M. Hodgson and Z. Irving, eds., 21–36. Bristol: Policy Press.

Jentoft, S., and A. Davis. 1993. Self and sacrifice: An investigation of small boat fisher individualism and its implication for producer cooperatives. *Human Organization* 52 (3): 356–367. DOI: 10.17730/humo.52.4.4650487532761447

Kanabishi, K. 2012. *3.11 dokoku no kiroku* [3.11 record of wails]. Tokyo: Shinyo-sha. [In Japanese]

Kase, K. 2012. Disaster damage of family based fishery and the feature of recovery policy. *Rekishi to keizai* 54 (3): 24–33. [In Japanese] DOI: 10.20633/rekishitokeizai.54.3_24

Kase, K. 2013. *Gyogyou "tokku," no naniga mondaika* [What is the problem of Fishery Special Zoning Policy?]. Tokyo: Gyokyo keieisentaa. [In Japanese]

Katayama, S. 2016. Recovery of the damaged fishery. In *Kiro ni tatsu shinsai hukko*. Hasegawa Koichi, Hobo Takehiko, and Ozaki Hironao, eds., 91–106. Tokyo: University of Tokyo Press. [In Japanese]

Kawaguchi, Y. 2019. A Kansaijin in Tohoku: Autoethnography on the recognition of self and others. *Japanese Journal of Cultural Anthropology* 84 (2): 153–171. [In Japanese] DOI: 10.14890/jjcanth.84.2_153.

Kawai, H., and S. Washida. 2010. *Rinshō to kotoba* [Clinic-ness and language]. Tokyo: Asahi bunko. [In Japanese]

Kawashima, S. 2015. Aspects of the recovering fishery communities from natural disaster: Sanriku and Great East Japan Earthquake. In *Saigai to sonraku*. Ueda Kyoko, ed., 119–147. Tokyo: Nobunkyo. [In Japanese]

Kelman, I. 2020. *Disaster by choice: How our actions turn natural hazards into catastrophes*. Oxford: Oxford University Press.

Kimura, S. 2013. *Shinsai no kōkyō jinruigaku* [Public anthropology of disaster]. Kyoto: Sekaishisosha. [In Japanese]

Kimura, T. 2016. Revival of local festivals and religion after the Great East Japan Earthquake. *Journal of Religion in Japan* 5 (2–3): 227–245. DOI: 10.1163/22118349-00502001.

Klein, N. 2011 (2007). *The shock doctrine: The rise of disaster capitalism*. Matsuhima Seiko, trans. Tokyo: Hamanosyuppan. [In Japanese]

Kodani, R. 2012. Report of disaster damage on intangible folk cultural properties in Miyagi. *Minzoku-geino kenkyu* 52: 31–51. [In Japanese]

Koester, D., and L. Niglas. 2011. Hunting in Itelmen: Filming a past practice in a disappearing language. *Sibirica* 10 (3): 55–81. DOI: 10.3167/sib.2011.100303.

Kruger, F., G. Bankoff, T. Cannon, B. Orlowski, and E. Schipper, eds. 2015. *Cultures and disasters: Understanding cultural framings in disaster risk reduction*. London and New York: Routledge.

Kulatunga, U. 2010. Impact of culture towards disaster risk reduction. *International Journal of Strategic Property Management* 14 (4): 304–313.

Kuwayama, T. 2004. *Native anthropology: The Japanese challenge to Western academic hegemony*. Melbourne: Trans Pacific Press.

Lahournat, F. 2016. Reviving tradition in disaster-affected communities: Adaptation and continuity in the kagura of Ogatsu, Miyagi Prefecture. *Contemporary Japan* 28 (2): 185–207.

Leibbrandt, A., U. Gneezy, and J. A. List. 2013. Rise and fall of competitiveness in individualistic and collectivistic societies. *PNAS* 110 (23): 9305–9308. DOI: 10.1073/pnas.1300431110.

Lindahl, K. 2007. Storms of memory: New Orleanians surviving Katrina in Houston. *Callaloo* 29 (4): 1526–1538.

Littlejohn, A. 2021. The potential of intangible loss: Reassembling heritage and reconstructing the social in post-disaster Japan. *Social Anthropology* 10: 1–16. DOI: 10.1111/1469-8676.13095.

Maki, N. 2015. Introduction: Disaster, disaster risk reduction in Asia. In *Kokusai kyoryoku to bosai*. M. Norio and Y. Hiroyuki, eds., 1–14. Kyoto: Kyoto University Press. [In Japanese]

Maki, N., and I. Hayashi. 1999. Disaster management in the Papua New Guinea tsunami disaster on 17 July, 1998. *Chiiki Anzen Gakkai Ronbunshū* 1: 195–200. [In Japanese]

Maki, N., and H. Yamamoto, eds. 2015. *Kokusai kyōryoku to bōsai* [International collaboration and disaster risk prevention]. Kyoto: Kyoto University Press. [In Japanese]

Marin, A. 2010. Riders under storms: Contributions of nomadic herders' observations to analysing climate change in Mongolia. *Global Environmental Change* 20 (1): 162–176. DOI: 10.1016/j.gloenvcha.2009.10.004

Mead, M. 1995. Visual anthropology in a discipline of words. In *Principles of visual Anthropology*. P. Hocking, ed., 3–10. Berlin: Mouton de Gruyter.

McNeil, D. 2013. Them vs us: Japanese and international reporting of the Fukushima nuclear crisis. In *Japan copes with calamity*. T. Gill, B. Steger, and D. Slater, eds., 127–150. Oxford: Peter Lang Publishing.

Merli, C. 2010. Context-bound Islamic theodicies: The tsunami as supernatural retribution vs. natural catastrophe in Southern Thailand. *Religion* 40: 104–111.

Michell, J. 1996. Ritual. In *Encyclopedia of social and cultural anthropology*. A. Barnard, and J. Spencer, eds., 490–493. London and New York: Routledge.

Minami, H., K. Ota, and M. Tanaka. 2011. The Great East Japan Earthquake and the activities asked of nursing academics now and in the future: JANA Report. *Trends in the Sciences* 16 (12): 82–86. [In Japanese] DOI: 10.5363/tits.16.12_82.

Molina, J. L., Lubbers, M. J., Valenzuela-Garcıa, H. and Gomez-Mestres, S. 2017. Cooperation and competition in social anthropology. *Anthropology Today* 33 (1): 11–14.

Morioka, R. 2013. Mother courage: Woman as activists between a passive populace and a paralyzed government. In *Japan copes with calamity*. T. Gill, B. Steger, and D. Slater, eds., 177–200. Oxford: Peter Lang Publishing.

Morris, J. F., and M. Ueyama. 2020. *An essay on the safeguard of historical archive and disaster aid*. [In Japanese]. http://hdl.handle.net/10097/00129482.

Nagano, Y. 2014. Depopulation, aging trends after the Great East Japan Earthquake in fishing communities: The case of Urato islands in Miyagi, Japan. *Sensyu ningen kagaku ronsyu, syakaigaku* 4: 119–135. [In Japanese]

Nihei, N. 2018. Neoliberalization and risk redistribution: For post-3.11 bio-politics. *Trends in Sciences* 18 (10): 59–63. [In Japanese] DOI: 10.5363/tits.18.10_59

Numazaki, I. 2012. Too wide, too big, too complicated to comprehend: A personal reflection on the disaster that started on March 11, 2011. *Asian Anthropology* 11: 1, 27–38. DOI: 10.1080/1683478X.2012.10600853

Obiya, H. 2016. Community-initiative recovery activities in the tsunami damaged fishery village and social capital. In *Kiro ni tatsu shinsai hukko*. Hasegawa

Koichi, Hobo Takehiko, and Ozaki Hironao, eds., 107–129. Tokyo: University of Tokyo Press. [In Japanese]

Ogawa, N. 1997. Inasaku [Rice farming]. In *Seigyō to minzoku*. Nomoto Hirokazu and Katsuki Yoichiro, eds., 19–51. Tokyo: Yūzankaku. [In Japanese]

Ohizumu, K. 2014. *Kibo no nihon nogyoron* [Agriculture of Japan from the hope perspective]. Tokyo: NHK Syuppan. [in Japanese]

Ohnuki-Tierney, E. 1993. *Rice as self: Japanese identities through time*. Princeton: Princeton University Press.

Oikawa, T. 2018. Okinawaken ni okeru hinansya ukeire katei [The process of acceptance of the evacuees in Okinawa]. In *Shinsaigo no chiiki bunka to hisaisya no minzokushi*. H. Takakura and M. Yamaguchi, eds., 252–263. Tokyo: Shinsensya. [In Japanese]

Oliver-Smith, A. 2009. Anthropology and the political economy of disasters. In *The political economy of hazards and disasters*. Eric C. Jones and A. D. Murphy, eds., 11–28. Lanham: Altamira Press.

Oliver-Smith, A. 2013a. A matter of choice. *International Journal of Disaster Risk Reduction* 3: 1–3.

Oliver-Smith, A. 2013b. Disaster risk reduction and climate change adaptation: The view from applied anthropology. *Human Organization* 72 (4): 275–282. DOI: 10.17730/humo.72.4.j7u8054266386822

Oliver-Smith, A. 2015. Hazards and disaster research in contemporary anthropology. In *International Encyclopedia of the Social & Behavioral Sciences*. DOI: 10.1016/b978-0-08-097086-8.12188–9

Ominami, J., Ando, K., Kikuchi, M., Harada, S., and Yamada, F. 2019. Fishermen's consciousness of the fishery revival district in Miyagi prefecture: The classification analysis of a questionnaire survey. *Kokusai gyogyo kenkyu* 17: 69–82. Nara: Japan International Fisheries Research Society. [In Japanese]

Oxley, M. C. 2013. A "people-centred principles-based" post-Hyogo framework to strengthen the resilience of national and communities. *International Journal of Disaster Risk Reduction* 4: 1–9. DOI: 10.1016/j.ijdrr.2013.03.004.

Pasupleti, R. S. 2013. Designing culturally responsive built environments in post disaster contexts. *International Journal of Disaster Risk Reduction* 6: 28–39. DOI: 10.1016/j.ijdrr.2013.03.008

Petryna, A. 1995. Sarcophagus: Chernobyl in historical light. *Cultural Anthropology* 10 (2): 196–220. DOI: 10.1525/can.1995.10.2.02a00030.

Petryna, A. 2016. *Life exposed: Biological citizens after Chernobyl*. Morimoto Maiko and Wakamatsu Fumitaka, trans. Kyoto: Jinbun Syoin. [In Japanese]

Pollnac, R. B. 1988. Social and cultural characteristics of fishing peoples. *Marine Behavior and Physiology* 14: 23–39. DOI: 10.1080/10236248809378691

Putnam, R. 1995. Bowling alone: America's declining social capital. *Journal of Democracy* 6(1): 65–78.

Ryugasaki, T. 2014. Formation of fishing rights and the Great East Japan Earthquake. *International Cultural Studies* 21: 109–133. Yokohama: Yokohama City University [In Japanese]

Sakaguchi, N. 2019. Post-disaster city reconstruction efforts and fishing villages transformation: Over tsunami disaster heritage. *Journal of Asian Rural Studies* 3 (2): 208–220. DOI: 10.20956/jars.v3i2.1910

Sasaki, K. 1993. *Ecology and stock property of the Sakhalin surf clam.* Tokyo: Nihon Suisan Shigen Hogo Kyoukai. [In Japanese]

Shaw, R., N. Uy, and J. Baumwoll. 2008. *Indigenous knowledge for disaster: Good practices and lessons from experiences in the Asia-Pacific region.* Bangkok: UN ISDR. Accessed 14 February 2022. www.unisdr.org/files/3646_Indigenous-KnowledgeDRR.pdf

Shibayama, A., and S. Boret. 2019. Transforming the archives of the Great East Japan Earthquake into global natural disaster archives. *IOP Conference Series: Earth & Environmental Science* 273 (1): 012039. DOI: 10.1088/1755-1315/273/1/012039.

Shimizu, A. 1992. The eternal primitive culture and peripheral peoples: A historical overview of modern Western anthropology. *Bulletin of National Museum of Ethnology.* Osaka 17 (3): 417–488. [In Japanese]

Shimizu, A. 2001. Nihon no jinruigaku: Kokusaiteki ichi to kanosei [Anthropology in Japan: An international position and the potential]. In *Jinruigaku-teki jissen no saikōchiku.* Takeshi Sugishima, ed., 172–203. Kyoto: Sekaishisosha. [In Japanese]

Shimizu, H. 2017. Reflections on the "anthropology of response-ability" through engagement. *Japanese Review of Cultural Anthropology* 18 (1): 5–36.

Shore, C. 2012. Anthropology and public policy. In *The SAGE handbook of social anthropology.* R. Fardon, ed. SAGE. DOI: 10.4135/9781446201077.n8

Shore, C., and S. Wright. 2011. Conceptualising policy: Technologies of governance and the politics of visibility. In *Policy worlds: Anthropology and the analysis of contemporary power.* Cris Shore and David Pero, eds., 1–25. New York: Berghahn Books.

Slator, D. 2015. Moralities of volunteer aid. In *Japan, copes with calamity.* T. Gill, B. Steger, and D. Slater, eds., 267–291. Oxford: Peter Lang.

Solnit, R. 2009. *A Paradise built in hell: Extraordinary communities that arise in a disaster.* New York: Penguin books.

Speranza, C., B. Kiteme, P. Ambenje, U. Wiesmann, and S. Makali. 2010. Indigenous knowledge related to climate variability and change. *Climate Change* 100: 295–315. DOI: 10.1007/s10584-009-9713-0

Suga, Y. 2013. 'Atarashii no no gakumon' no jidai e [Toward the new humanities outside of academia]. Tokyo: Iwanamishoten. [In Japanese]

Sugawara, D., F. Imamura, and K. Goto. 2013. The 2011 Tohoku-oki earthquake tsunami: Similarities and differences to the 869 Jogan Tsunami on the Sendai Plain. *Pure and Applied Geophysics* 170: 831–843. DOI: 10.1007/s00024-012-0460-1

Sugiyama, K. 1967. A comparative study of rice rites in central India and Japan. *Nihon bunka kenkyūjo hōkoku* 3: 111–292. Sendai: Tohoku University. [In Japanese]

Suzuki, I. 2012. Concepts on the dead as seen in the choice of ground burials during the Great East Japan earthquake. In *Fukkō to saisei e no teigen. 1.* Yutaka Zakoda, ed., 103–121. Sendai: Tohoku University Press. [In Japanese]

Suzuki, Y. 2012. Social demand level of hazard estimation and responsibility. *Trends in the Sciences* 17 (8): 20–24. [In Japanese] DOI: 10.5363/tits.17.8_20.

Takahashi, M. 2015. Conservation policy of salmon fishing in 19th century Sendai clan. In *Edo jidai no seiji to ciikishakai, nikan, Chiikisyakai to bunka*. Hirakawa Arata, ed., 187–213. Osaka: Seibundo. [In Japanese]

Takakura, H., and S. Boret. 2021. The value of visual disaster records from digital archives and films in Post-3/11 Japan. *International Journal of Sustainable Future for Human Security* 7 (3): 58–65. DOI: 10.24910/jsustain/7.3/5865

Takakura, H., and T. Kimura, eds. 2012. *Kikigaki shinsai taiken, tohoku daigaku 90nin ga kataru 3.11* [Recordings of disaster experiences: Interviews of 90 Tohoku University people on the 3.11 disaster]. Tokyo: Shinsensha. [In Japanese]

Takakura, H., and K. Takizawa, eds. 2013. *Survey on Miyagi prefecture coastal area folk cultural assets damaged by the Great East Japan Earthquake (Collected reports 2012)*. Sendai: Tohoku University Center for Northeast Asian Studies. [In Japanese]

Takakura, H., and K. Takizawa, eds. 2014. *Mukei minzoku bunkazai ga hisai suru toiukoto* [What intangible cultural heritage is damaged: The Great East Japan Earthquake and ethnographies of regional society in Miyagi Prefecture's coastline]. Tokyo: Shinsensha. [In Japanese]

Takakura, H., K. Takizawa, and N. Masaoka, eds. 2012. *Survey on miyagi prefecture coastal area folk cultural assets damaged by the Great East Japan Earthquake (Collected reports 2011)*. Sendai: Tohoku University Center for Northeast Asian Studies. [In Japanese]

Takakura, H., and M. Yamaguchi, eds. 2018. *Shinsaigo no chiiki bunka to hisaisya no minzokusi* [Ethnographies of local cultures and victims after the disaster]. Tokyo: Shinsensha. [In Japanese]

Takakuwa, M. 1994. *Nihon gyomin syakairon kou: Minzokugakuteki kenkyu* [A thought on Japanese fishery societies]. Tokyo: Miraisha. [In Japanese]

Takano, T. 2013. Current condition and tasks of the tsunami disaster recovery of coastal fishing: A case of Hirota bay. *Chiiki kosougaku kenkyu kyoiku hokoku* 4: 1–21. [In Japanese]

Takeuchi, T. 1976 (1959). Inasaku [Rice farming]. In *Seigyō no minzoku*. Ohmachi Tokuzō, Oka Masao, Sakurada Katsunori, Seki Keigo, and Mogami Takayoshi, eds., 13–48. Tokyo: Heibonsha. [In Japanese]

Takezawa, S. 2013. *Hisaigo wo ikiru: Kirikiri, Ootsuchi, Kamaichi huntoki* [Living after the disaster: Recovery reports of Kirikiri, Ootsuchi, Kamaishi]. Tokyo: Chuokoronsha. [In Japanese]

Takezawa, S. 2016. *The aftermath of the 2011 East Japan earthquake and tsunami: Living among the rubble*. P. Barton, trans. Lanham: Lexington Books.

Takizawa, K. 2014. The reconstruction of community and the persistence of festivals after the Great East Japan Earthquake. *Shūkyō kenkyū* 87: 436–437. [In Japanese] DOI: 10.20716/rsjars.87.Suppl_436

Takizawa, K. 2019. Resilience of communities affected by the Great East Japan Earthquake and restoration of their local festivals. In *Crisis and disaster in Japan and New Zealand*. S. Bouterey and L. E. Marceau, eds., 41–57. Singapore: Palgrave Macmillan.

Tatsumi, Y. 2014. Hinan ga umidasu heiwa: genpatsu jiko kara no boshi hinansya ga tsukuridasu aratana kizuna [The peace through the evacuation: New social tie for the mother – child evacuees from Fukushima accident]. In *Heiwa no Jinruigaku*. H. Oda, ed., 187–209. Kyoto: Horitsu Bunkasya. [In Japanese]

Testart, A. 1995. *Les chasseurs-cueilleurs ou l'origine des inégalités*. Yamauchi Hisashi, ed. Tokyo: Hosei University Press. [In Japanese]

TU. 2013. *Tohoku University records of the great East Japan earthquake*. Sendai: Tohoku University. [In Japanese]. www.bureau.tohoku.ac.jp/somu/shinsai/shinsai_kiroku.pdf.

TUSM. 2012. *Tohoku University School of Medicine records of the great East Japan earthquake*. Sendai: Tohoku University. [In Japanese]. Accessed 14 February 2023. https://www.med.tohoku.ac.jp/d_report/report/

Uchio, T. 2016. NGO activity as a method for public anthropology: From a case study of disaster-relief activities in Miyagi prefecture. *Reitaku Daigaku Journal* 99: 1–9.

Uchio, T. 2018. *Fukko to songen* [Dignity after 3.11 disaster]. Tokyo: Tokyo University Press. [In Japanese]

Uchiyamada, Y. 2017. Invisible radiation and words of assurance in Fukushima. *Rekishi Jinrui* 45: 1–19. [In Japanese] http://hdl.handle.net/2241/00146493.

Ueda, K. 2013. Why do sufferers of Great Earthquake conduct the traditional events? [In Japanese]. *Shakaigaku Nenpo* 42: 43–60. DOI: 10.11271/tss.42.43.

Ueda, K., and H. Torigoe. 2012. Why do victims of the tsunami return to the coast? *International Journal of Japanese Sociology* 21: 21–29. DOI: 10.1111/j.1475-6781. 2012.01159.x

UNESCO. 2018. *Basic texts of the 2003 convention for the safeguarding of the intangible cultural heritage*. Paris: UNESCO.

UNISDR. 2015. *Sendai framework for disaster risk reduction 2015–30*. Accessed 1 August 2017. www.unisdr.org/files/43291_sendaiframeworkfordrren.pdf

Watanabe, A. 2005. The aesthetics of paddy fields. *Bulletin of Japanese Folklore Studies* 242: 64–79. [In Japanese]

Watanabe, A. 2011. How to evaluate failures? The process of developing technologies in the modernization of rice farming. *Bulletin of the National Museum of Japanese History* 162: 223–238. [In Japanese]

Watanabe, H. 1986. Occupational differentiation and social stratification: The case of northern Pacific maritime food gatherers. *Current Anthropology* 24 (2): 217–219.

Watari. 1977. *Watari choushi. gekan* [History of Watari township]. Watari: Watari-cho. [In Japanese]

Westlund, L., F. Poulin, H. Bage, and R. van Anrooy. 2007. *Disaster response and risk management in fisheries sector*. Rome: FAO.

Wilhelm, J. 2018. Seven years after disaster: Fisheries communities in coastal Pacific Tōhoku. In *small-scale fisheries in Japan: Environmental and sociocultural perspectives*. Giovanni Bulian and Yasushi Nakano, eds., 129–151. Venezia: Edizioni Ca'Foscari. DOI: 10.30687/978-88-6969-226-0/006

Wilhelm, J., and A. E. Delaney. 2013. No homes, no boats, no rafts: Miyagi coastal people in the aftermath of disaster. In *Japan, copes with calamity*. T. Gill, B. Steger, and D. Slater, eds., 99–124. Oxford: Peter Lang.

Wood, D. C. 2012. Tremors in the "contact zone" and challenges to anthropology following the Great East Japan Earthquake. *Asian Anthropology* 11 (1): 39–53

Yamaguchi, M. 2016. Things beyond or within the border: Local correspondence against radiation in Hippo village, Marumori. *Tohoku Bunka Kenyushitsu Kiyo* 57: 23–39. [In Japanese]. http://hdl.handle.net/10097/00121489.

Yamaguchi, Y. 2011 (1943). *Tsunami to mura* [Tsunami and villages]. Masami Ishii Masami and Shūichi Kawashima, eds. Tokyo: Miyai Shoten. [In Japanese]

Yamakawa, F. 2012. The severe accident of Tokyo electric power company Fukushima Daiichi Nuclear Power Plant and restoration of Fukushima. *Trends in the Sciences* 17 (8): 26–31. [In Japanese] DOI: 10.5363/tits.17.8_26.

Yamamoto. 1994. *On a placename of Yamamotocho*. Yamamoto: Yamamotochou kyoiku iinkai. [In Japanese]

Yamamoto. 2018a. *Report of Yamamoto township recovery from disaster*. [In Japanese]. Accessed 1 June 2019. www.town.yamamoto.miyagi.jp/site/fukkou/8629.html

Yamamoto. 2018b. *Yamamoto township recovery master plan, appendix 1 basic date*. [In Japanese]. Accessed 8 August 2019. https://town.yamamoto.miyagi.jp/uploaded/attachment/7365.pdf

Yamashita, S. 2012. The public anthropology of disaster. *Asian Anthropology* 11 (1): 21–25.

Yamauchi, M. 2012. Direct seeding of rice crop in flooded paddy field using iron-coated seeds. *Japanese Journal of Crop Science* 81 (2): 148–159. [In Japanese] DOI: 10.1626/jcs.81.148

Yanagida, K. 1969 (1955). Ine to mizu [Rice and water]. In *Ine no nihonshi, jō*. Yanagida Kunio, Ando Kotaro, and Morinaga Shuntaro, eds., 60–96. Tokyo: Chikuma shobō. [In Japanese]

Yasumuro, S. 2012. *Nihon minzoku seigyō ron* [Japanese folklore and subsistence]. Tokyo: Keiyūsha.

Yoshino, K. 2017. TURFs in the post-quake recovery: Case studies in Sanriku fishing communities, Japan. *Marine Policy* 86: 47–55. DOI: 10.1016/j.marpol.2017.08.029

Young, O. R., F. Berkhout, G. C. Gallopin, M. Janssen, E. Ostrom, and S. Van Der Leeuw. 2006. The globalization of socio-ecological systems: An agenda for scientific research. *Global Environmental Change* 16 (3): 304–316. DOI: 10.1016/j.gloenvcha.2006.03.004

Index

Note: Page numbers in *italic* type indicate figures and page numbers in **bold** type indicate charts.

3.11 disaster: components of 1; Great East Japan Earthquake 10, 11–12; prefectures affected by 29; timing of, in relation to Tohoku University 21–22; *see also* Fukushima Daiichi Nuclear Power Plant; tsunami (2011)

Adachi, Mr. (pseud.) 57, 61, 64, 70, 74
anthropologists and anthropology: colonial anthropology 33; ethnographic rescue as foundation of 32; ethnographists and ethnography compared to 12; evaluation of culture 4; expertise of, in field of intangible cultural heritage 36, 37; fieldwork as building long-term relationships 35, 36–37; fieldwork tasks 34; Japanese, described 4; methodology of 9, 36–37; and plans for disaster risk reduction 38; as slow science 4, 28; systematic explanation of 33; views of existing disciplines used by 34; visual 33–34
Aoki, Tamotsu 35

Beck, Ulrich 42
"biological citizenship" 42
biological response knowledge 77, 78

cage fishing 83, 86, 88, 89–90, 91, **92**
Cartier-Bresson, Henri 33

chokuha direct seeding technique of rice planting 61, 62, 74, 75
collaboration *see* cooperation
colonial anthropology 33
communitas, sense of 44
community involvement: as feature of intangible cultural heritage 40; *shishimai* dance 44; street associations 44
competitiveness: and allocation for sedentary fish with low resource fluctuation 7; among plants in rice fields 66; coexistence of cooperation and, in fishery communities 82, 86, *87*, 88, 92, 93–94, 95, 96n7; factors leading to 81; and individualism in fishery communities 80, 81, 92; and recovery 93
contemporary settings, as feature of intangible cultural heritage 40
cooperation: coexistence of competitiveness and, in fishery communities 82, 86, *87*, 88, 92, 93–94, 95, 96n7; and community resilience 81; and "disaster utopia" concept 80–81; in fishing 85–86, 88–89, 90–92; and individualism after disasters 81; and necessity of solidarity 93; and social capital 81
culture: anthropoligists' evaluation of 4; differences among localities 9–10; and disaster risk reduction 2–3; as lens for disasters 2

For Product Safety Concerns and Information please contact our EU
representative GPSR@taylorandfrancis.com
Taylor & Francis Verlag GmbH, Kaufingerstraße 24, 80331 München, Germany

www.ingramcontent.com/pod-product-compliance
Lightning Source LLC
Chambersburg PA
CBHW071053280326
41928CB00050B/2478